THE PARADOXES OF ACTION

Law and Philosophy Library

VOLUME 67

THE PARADOXES OF ACTION

Human Action, Law and Philosophy

by

DANIEL GONZÁLEZ LAGIER

Professor of Legal Theory,
University of Alicante,
Alicante, Spain

KLUWER ACADEMIC PUBLISHERS
DORDRECHT / BOSTON / LONDON

A C.I.P. Catalogue record for this book is available from the Library of Congress.

ISBN 978-90-481-6443-1

Published by Kluwer Academic Publishers,
P.O. Box 17, 3300 AA Dordrecht, The Netherlands.

Sold and distributed in North, Central and South America
by Kluwer Academic Publishers,
101 Philip Drive, Norwell, MA 02061, U.S.A.

In all other countries, sold and distributed
by Kluwer Academic Publishers,
P.O. Box 322, 3300 AH Dordrecht, The Netherlands.

Translated from the Spanish
by Ruth Zimmerling

Printed on acid-free paper

Printed in the Netherlands.

For Merche

TABLE OF CONTENTS

Foreword *by Manuel Atienza* 1

Preface 7

Chapter I. Preliminaries

1. The Concept of Action and the Traps of Language 11
2. The Relevance of the Concept of Human Action for Ethics and the Law 13
3. Human Freedom as a Prerequisite 15

Chapter II: Our Intuitions and the Paradoxes of Action

1. Introduction 17
2. First Paradox: Are Actions Natural Phenomenoa or Products of Our Worldview? 19
3. Second Paradox: Are Actions Bodily Movements or Descriptions of Bodily Movements? 19
4. Third Paradox: Can We Be Mistaken About Our Own Actions? 20
5. Fourth Paradox: Do We Perform Several Actions With One Single Bodily Movement? (The 'Accordion Effect' of Actions) 21
6. Fifth Paradox: What Are the Limits of Our Actions? 22

Chapter III: The Debate in the Philosophy of Action

1. The Controversy About the Individuation of Actions 23
   1. The minimizing position 24 / 2. The maximizing position 26
2. Individuation From the Agent's Point of View (G. H. von Wright) 30
3. Individuation as Imputation (H. L. A. Hart) 32
4. Some Conclusions 36

CHAPTER IV: THE DEBATE IN CRIMINAL LAW

1. Introduction 39

2. The Definition of 'Action' in Criminal-Law Doctrine 40

1. The causal theory of action. The trilemma of causalism 40 / 2. The teleological theory of action. The partial abandoning of teleology 43 / 3. The social theory of action. Its insufficiency 44 / 4. A new version of the social theory: the theory of action as meaning 46

3. The Treatment of Action in Anglo-Saxon Law 49

1. *Act requirement* and *actus reus requirement*. The orthodox theory of action 50 / 2. Objectivism vs. subjectivism 52

4. Conclusions 53

CHAPTER V: THE DEBATE IN THE PHILOSOPHY OF LANGUAGE

1. Introduction. Good Times for Pragmatics 55

2. Language Games (Wittgenstein) 56

3. An Intentional Theory of Meaning (H. P. Grice) 58

1. The reconstruction of semantic concepts from pragmatic concepts 58 / 2. The role of conventions in the determination of meaning 60 / 3. Searle's critique of the conception of Grice 61

4. How To Do Things With Words (J. L. Austin) 62

1. 'Constative utterances' and 'performative utterances' 62 / 2. 'Locutionary acts', 'illocutionary acts', and 'perlocutionary acts' 64

5. An Integrative Theory of Speech Acts (J. Searle) 69

1. Introduction 69 / 2. Rules and speech acts. The structure of illocutionary acts 70 / 3. 'A taxonomy of illocutionary acts' 72 / 4. Intention and illocutionary acts 76

6. Conclusions 77

CHAPTER VI: THE PARADOXES DISSOLVED

1. Recapitulation. The Aspects of Action 79

1. Naturalistic, subjectivist, and social theories of action 79 / 2. The complementariness of the three groups of theories. Basic act, result-act and consequence-act. Act and action 80 / 3. The aspects of action and the distinction between locutionary, illocutionary, and perlocutionary acts 81 / 4. Criteria for the distinction between the three aspects of action 82

2. The Paradoxes of Action Reconsidered 85

1. Solution of the first paradox 86 / 2. Solution of the second paradox 86 / 3. Solution of the third paradox 86 / 4. Solution of the fourth paradox 87 / 5. Solution of the fifth paradox 87

CHAPTER VII: THE STRUCTURE OF ACTION

1. Introduction 91

2. The Sequence of Bodily Movements 91

   1. The role of bodily movements 91 / 2. Any bodily movement? 92 / 3. Limits of bodily movements 93

3. Changes in the World 93

   1. Do all actions bring about a change in the world? 93 / 2. 'Action-internal' change 93 / 3. Natural changes and institutional changes 94 / 4. From one world to the other 94 / 5. Any change? 94

4. The Link Between a Bodily Movement and a Change in the World 96

   1. Causal relations 96 / 2. Conventional relations 97 / 3. Relations of implication? 97

5. Intention 98

   1. Intentionality and Intention 98 / 2. Do intentions exist in the mind? Volitionists and anti-volitionists 99 / 3. Intentions and wants 101 / 4. Intention prior to action, and intention in acting 103 / 5. Internal (subjective) intention and external (objective) intention 104 / 6. Voluntariness and intention 106

6. The Interpretation or Meaning of an Action 107

   1. What does 'meaning of an action' mean? 107 / 2. The intentional interpretation of bodily movements 109 / 3. The non-intentional interpretation of bodily movements 112

CHAPTER VIII: OTHER KINDS OF ACTIONS

1. Introduction 115

2. Institutional Actions 115

   1. John Searle's distinction between natural and institutional actions 115 / 2. Two kinds of institutional actions 116

3. Remarks on Omission 117

   1. Omission and bodily movements 118 / 2. Omission and changes in the world 119 / 3. Omission and links 119 / 4. Omission and intention 120 / 5. Omission and interpretation 120

EPILOGUE 123

BIBLIOGRAPHY 127

INDEX OF NAMES 135

FOREWORD

Through the combined effects of certain natural facts (connected with the passage of time), institutional acts (performed at various points within the university system) and bonds of friendship (forged over quite a number of years of academic life), I have lately become an occasional writer of forewords. It is certainly not a kind of work that displeases me; but it would be too much to say that I have learned to do it with ease. Quite to the contrary!

Writing a foreword is, it seems to me, an example of a rather complex action (although, of course, much less complex than writing the book it accompanies). In fact, it is not even an action; it is rather an activity, carried out over a more or less prolonged period of time and typically including something like the following stages: deciding to write the foreword; carefully reading the book; taking notes; thinking about what would be appropriate aspects to be mentioned; sketching an outline; writing a first draft by hand; writing several corrected versions; typing the last of them into the computer; distributing it to several colleagues to see how they like it; correcting the text once more; sending it to the author of the book; delivering it to the publisher. In each of these actions (leaving aside for a moment purely mental actions such as thinking) we can in turn distinguish several components. These are, basically: bodily movements, intentions, and (intentionally or unintentionally produced) changes in the world.

For instance, the action of writing the first draft (or, for simplicity's sake, one of the paragraphs of the first draft) of the present foreword consisted, to begin with, in certain bodily movements (of my hand grabbing a pen and gliding over a piece of paper) which I carried out voluntarily (no-one guided my hand). Secondly, there are some changes in the world which I intended to produce and which also seem to form part of that action: the appearance on the paper (following certain laws of physics) of ink spots distributed in a certain pattern; or the production (by virtue of the syntactic and semantic rules of the Spanish language) of a text with a meaning (or perhaps even several meanings). And, finally, there may be still other changes which I did not intend and the production of which I did not foresee, but which, nevertheless, also form part of that same action. For example, because I concentrated so hard on the formulation of my text, I did not realize that I was writing on a piece of paper on which my son Miguel had drawn a picture, with the effect that when he discovered my terrible mistake he started crying desperately. Or perhaps (and that is actually partly true) because, although I had wanted to write a foreword that would please Daniel and that he could even regard as a kind of wedding present (as I began to write the first draft a few days before the author of this book, in a joint action with Mercedes, set out to bring about an – institutional – change in the world consisting in raising by two the number of married persons), what happened was that he was offended by the paragraph in question and decided that his book should be published without a foreword after all.

Seriously speaking, the example of writing a foreword can serve perfectly well for a quick review of the kinds of problems and questions treated in this book: Are actions (writing a foreword) phenomena that exist (and that we can observe) just like physical objects, or are they rather a way of seeing the world, a kind of interpretation? Should we regard actions as bodily movements (my hand grabbing the pen), or rather as *descriptions* of bodily movements (which vary from one observer to the next: destroying a picture, scribbling on paper, writing a foreword, ...)? How could it be possible that someone who performs an action does not know what he is doing? Or do we always know? How many actions did I perform when I wrote the paragraph? Was offending Daniel one of them? And did I also perform the action of bringing about that the foreword it cost me so much effort to write will remain unpublished?

González Lagier's strategy for answering these questions is, at the same time, simple and effective. He begins by giving a summary of the current debate in the philosophy of action which leads him to the conclusion that a good part of the controversies in that field are more apparent than real. As he sees it, the different theories about action he reviews (and which are, in fact, the most relevant) are not about the same subject; rather, they refer each to a different one of the several aspects we can distinguish in actions, i. e. to bodily movements (the natural dimension), to what is intentionally done in carrying out those bodily movements (the subjective dimension), and to the socially relevant consequences this may produce (the social dimension).

If one examines – as González Lagier does next – the situation in the field of criminal dogmatics, one can draw an analogous conclusion: the causal theory, the teleological theory, and the social theory of action all share the characteristic of reducing the phenomenon of action to only one of its three basic elements. Rather than as three rival theories, one can therefore regard them as complementary theories about different subjects, namely, about what the author calls the 'basic act', the 'result-act', and the 'consequence-act', respectively.

Finally, the third and last of González Lagier's theoretical explorations concerns the philosophy of language, and in particular Austin's distinction of locutionary act (the act of uttering something: for instance, 'Daniel is getting married on May 1'), illocutionary act (what one does by uttering something: telling Carmen about it), and perlocutionary act (the consequences of uttering something: provoking in Carmen – and myself – a feeling of sadness for not being able to assist at the wedding). In his view, if interpreted in a certain fashion, this distinction can be carried over from speech acts to actions in general, so that in the end we are back again at the distinction between physical movements, their intended results, and their social consequences.

Starting from this schema, which the author develops with a degree of detail and sophistication that I cannot do justice to here, the answer to the questions posed above is the following: If by an action one understands the basic act, then actions are natural phenomena. If, instead, an action is understood as an act-result or an act-consequence, then it is rather an 'interpretive attitude'. And that is why one and the same bodily movement (basic act) can give rise to different actions (interpretations), and one and the same kind of action (writing a foreword) can be performed through different bodily movements (the movement of my hand grabbing the pen, or the movements of my fingers hitting the keys of a keyboard; in other cases, the differences between bodily movements may even be much greater: one can kill another by firing a gun, by poisoning, by strangling, ...). An agent cannot be mistaken about his own actions if by action we understand the act-result (one cannot write a foreword without knowing it); an observer, in contrast, may be mistaken about it (someone might think I am writing a letter). With one single sequence of bodily movements I performed (according to the above description) several act-results (the changes in the world which I intended to bring about) plus an undetermined number of act-consequences. And concerning the question whether (sticking with the above example) the action of offending Daniel or of not getting this foreword published can be imputed to me, the answer is not (and cannot be) straightforward: it depends on criteria such as the distance in the causal chain between the bodily movements and the consequences, the existence of other events that might strengthen the causal chain (suppose I had recently started to criticize several aspects of Daniel's conduct), or the predictability and relevance of the consequence in question.

The most original – and the most important – part of the book begins once all these problems, which the author literally calls 'The Paradoxes of Action', have been resolved (approximately in the way I have just sketched). On that basis, Chapter VII then offers an analysis of the structure of action, taking into account the following five elements: the sequence of bodily movements, the effect or change in the world, the link between that sequence of bodily movements and the change in the world (or between one change and another), the intention, and the interpretation or meaning of the sequence of bodily movements. Chapter VIII, finally, focuses on two kinds of actions which are of particular interest in law: institutional actions (such as getting married, or pronouncing a sentence, which can only be performed because there are norms – constitutive norms – by virtue of which certain bodily movements 'count as' an action of marriage or of sentencing), and omissions.

Together, these two final chapters contain the fundamental elements of a theory of action, focusing primarily (but not exclusively) on the field of law. The author does not claim that this is already a full-fledged theory. Rather, it is presented as a first sketch which still needs to be adjusted here and there and, above all, to be developed further. I therefore dare to formulate a few suggestions which may perhaps be useful to González Lagier for another book hopefully to be published before long, in which he will offer us his (fully developed) theory of action, and of legal actions. I know that nothing I am going to say will be new to the author, but insistence sometimes bears fruit, and, in any case, the problems underlying these suggestions are fundamental enough to deserve the effort of yet another reflection on them.

My first suggestion concerns the distinction between basic act, act-result and act-consequence which, as we have seen, plays a central role in González Lagier's argument. Despite its apparent simplicity, it seems to me that this distinction still contains a measure of ambiguity that needs to be eliminated. To put it briefly, 'act' does not seem to mean the same in the three terms: in the first case, it refers exclusively to a kind of reality (a physical reality: bodily movements), whereas in the other two cases it not only denotes a kind of reality, but also a kind of interpretation; that is, the status of act-results and act-consequences is ambiguous because it is not clear whether they belong to or take place in the world or in language. In other words, it is not clear whether we are dealing with three *kinds* of acts (it seems not; but then speaking of 'act-result' and 'act-consequence' is confusing), with three *aspects* of acts (but these three aspects – if by 'aspect' one understands the ingredients or elements of actions – would have to be bodily movements, intentions, and changes in the world), or with two *interpretations* of one single act. This ambiguity allows the author to solve (or rather: dissolve) the problems we saw earlier, but he may be paying a price for that. It is not clear, for example, how intention prior to bodily movements could be made to fit into this schema (because it does not seem to form part of the basic act, nor of the act-result or the act-consequence). In fact, one has the impression that when in Chapter VII the author analyzes the structure of action, in a way he abandons his schema. I also think that the way how he solves the problem of the link between bodily movements and changes in the world is not entirely satisfactory. If, on the one hand, basic acts are what gives rise to changes in the world, but, on the other, these changes are what enables us to individuate basic acts, is this not somehow circular? Does it really make sense to speak of a 'conceptual' or 'internal connection' with regard to the link between an act and its consequence (in contrast to von Wright, González Lagier holds that not only results, but also consequences have that kind of relationship with an action, i. e., with a basic act)? How can the notion of a 'change internal to the action' (ch. VI, sect. 2.5.1) fulfil the function of individuating basic acts if it does not come provided with clear criteria which tell us when we are dealing with one of these 'internal changes'?

My second suggestion is that a theory of action, or of legal actions, should perhaps be linked more closely to the theory of legal norms, or legal sentences. In my view, that could help to clarify two very important questions mentioned several times in the present book.

The first of these questions concerns the existence of two basic ways of understanding or structuring actions: either in a classificatory or in a teleological way. With regard to the interpretation or the meaning of an action, for example, González Lagier distinguishes between a teleological interpretation (that is, an interpretation focusing on the agent's goal or purpose) and a hermeneutic interpretation (where to understand an action is – here, he follows von Wright – to classify it), and gives priority to the latter because it implies a broader concept of meaning, since it allows us to attribute meaning even to non-intentional actions (which, obviously, cannot be interpreted in teleological terms). However, I think that the question is not to choose between the two, but to recognize that there are two basic ways of structuring behaviour, which are reflected in the distinction we can draw between two kinds of regulatory norms, to wit, those referring to the action in classificatory terms (action norms) and those referring to it in teleological terms (end norms). The meaning of actions thus becomes relative to the kind of norm under which the action is considered. In the last instance, as has often been said, norms are schemata for the interpretation of actions.

The second question concerns the notion of institutional action. In my view, González Lagier gives an excessively broad meaning to that kind of action (which is to be distinguished from natural actions). This leads him to assert, for instance, that committing murder is an institutional act just like getting married because in both cases there is an institutional change (the legal situation of a murderer as well as of people who are getting married changes). The problem is that if we accepted this, then all actions regulated by legal norms would, I think, be institutional actions and the concept as such would lose its sense (to speak of 'institutional act-results' and 'institutional act-consequences' does not solve this problem, because that is a distinction within the category of institutional actions). In this case too, it seems to me, the distinction between regulatory legal norms and constitutive legal norms could be of help, as institutional actions may be understood as those actions which are subject to regulation by constitutive norms (or by a certain type of constitutive norms).

I have reserved until the end the section of praise which, especially in a case like this, is the easiest – and most pleasant – part of the definitely complex action of writing a foreword. From the very first page, the reader of this book will find that it is a mature work that is, moreover, clearly and elegantly written. If one adds to this the fact that it treats one of the most difficult topics one can imagine, one cannot but feel admiration and gratefulness. The concept of action (or, better perhaps, the family of concepts related with action) occupies a central position in the study of law as well as of many philosophical questions. But one rarely finds an analysis of these concepts which takes into account – as this book does – both the legal and the philosophical tradition. This is, therefore, a work that will interest lawyers and philosophers alike. And it is a magnificent example of what the philosophy of law ought to be: an activity aimed at connecting legal knowledge with the rest of social knowledge.

All these aspects, together with the fact that I have known Daniel González Lagier for a long time, induce me to end this foreword with a most summary judgement: An excellent book, written by an excellent person!

Ithaca, N. Y.
May 1, 2001 Manuel
Atienza

PREFACE

1. One frequently encounters concepts which do not seem to pose any problems at first sight, but turn out to be extremely elusive when one tries to pin them down with some precision. They are just like those distant nebulae we sometimes see in the sky: when we first lay our eyes on them we think we see them clearly; but when we keep staring we find that we are incapable of counting the stars they consist of. For philosophers, such concepts are at once frustrating and fascinating. One of them – surely one of the most frustrating and fascinating – is, no doubt, the concept of action.

In dealing with such concepts, we can ask ourselves what we should do about them – what philosophy should do to clarify them. An interesting answer to this question has been given by Friedrich Waismann, in an essay in which he explains his view of philosophy. Following the second Wittgenstein's conception of philosophy, Waismann recommends that rather than attempting to find a *solution* for these problems we should try to find an *explanation* for them. „A philosophical question – he says – is not solved: it *dis*solves". It dissolves when we recognize the traps language holds for us, bring them to light, and clarify the meaning of words to such an extent that we can release ourselves „from the spell [the question] casts on us".[1]

Following Waismann's suggestion, in this book I will venture on a course that may help to release us from the spell of (some of the words of) action. Of course, the concept of action also poses philosophical problems that go far beyond mere linguistic misunderstandings. But certainly it seems advisable to begin by clarifying the latter.

In this undertaking, I will be guided by two distinctions. The first is one of the most illuminating contributions we owe to John L. Austin, probably the philosopher of ordinary language who most thoroughly applied this philosophical method. I am, of course, referring to his distinction of the *locutionary*, the *illocutionary*, and the *perlocutionary* aspects of speech acts. The second distinction I take from an author who, quite to the contrary, has understood philosophy as a task of logical and formal analysis rather than of the analysis of ordinary language. That author is Georg Henrik von Wright, and I am here referring to his distinction between the *result* of an action and its *consequences*. One of the purposes of this book is to take Austin's tripartite classification of speech acts as a model for the construction of a similar – though in important aspects different – scheme that can be applied to other kinds of action, precisely in order to complement and reinterpret von Wright's distinction. I will show that by proceeding in this way it is possible to get rid of some counterintuitive aspects of the concept of action (in other words, of what I will call the 'paradoxes of action') and to see the debates of philosophers of action and legal philosophers in a new light.

[1] Waismann 1968, p. 10.

2. It may be helpful to begin with a few remarks on method. A *first* source of knowledge that may be useful for an investigation of the concept of action are our intuitions. With this, I do not mean to endorse an intuitionist theory of knowledge. I only wish to draw attention to the fact that in the case of the concept of action (which leads us to other concepts, such as intention, belief, desire, etc., that often refer to mental, i. e., internal, states) intuition can be particularly valuable as a means to finding at least some starting points. Besides, our intuitions are (or at least ought to be) parallel to the conclusions we can draw from the study of ordinary language, since they should enter into it. Recourse to ordinary language may be plagued by its own problems, but surely one cannot deny that there is some value in what Austin said in defence of this method (precisely concerning the concept of action):

„[...] our common stock of words embodies all the distinctions men have found worth drawing, and the connexions they have found worth making, in the lifetimes of many generations: they surely are likely to be more numerous, more sound, since they have stood up to the long test of the survival of the fittest, and more subtle, at least in all ordinary and reasonably practical matters, than any that you or I are likely to think up in our armchairs of an afternoon – the most favoured alternative method."[2]

A *second* source of information on the concept of action are the investigations of philosophers who have worked on this subject. Many of these investigations are indeed based on the study of ordinary language (e. g., those by Austin) or at least take it into account. But one can also find discussions, suggestions and conceptions of philosophers who go beyond ordinary language (and who, in any case, offer us a wealth of analytical work already done). Basically, and with the simplification always implied in such distinctions, we can say that contributions from the *philosophy of action* comprise *(1)* investigations of the concept and the structure of action, *(2)* investigations of the typical pattern or model of explanations of action, and *(3)* investigations of the rationality conditions of action. The first refer to such concepts as bodily movements, simple and complex actions, intention, description of actions, etc. The primary emphasis of the second is on the relationship between intention and action, and what is debated here is whether this relationship is of a causal or of some other nature (if the former, action could be explained by general laws just like other physical events; if the latter, action would not belong to the world of causality). The third group, finally, studies the kinds of reasons, desires, preferences, etc., that make our actions rational[3] – regardless of whether or not they are causally connected to action. In this book, I will be interested primarily in the first group of investigations. But obviously the three groups are strongly connected.

And the tree of philosophy has yet another branch which has carried fruit that may be useful for our investigation, although traditionally it has been regarded as altogether different from the branch of the philosophy of action. I am thinking of speech-act theory in general, and that famous distinction proposed by John L. Austin and already

[2] Austin 1979a, p. 182.

[3] Here, 'rational' can be understood in the broad sense – not restricted to the relationship between ends and means – which may include, for example, a moral rationality. Practical philosophy would then be a branch of the philosophy of action.

mentioned above, between locutionary, illocutionary and perlocutionary acts, in particular. As speech-act theory is a theory about a particular type of actions, there must necessarily exist some analogies between this particular theory and the theory of action in general.[4]

Finally, there are several reasons why the concept of action is interesting for lawyers. Law and legal science are thus the *third* source of knowledge to which special attention must be paid in any attempt to clarify the concept of action.[5] In the continental legal tradition, the study of the concept of action has been pursued mainly in the criminal law, which has elaborated three classical theories of action (the causal theory, the intentionalist theory, and the social theory) and has dealt with a number of problems (such as the individuation of actions in order to solve cases of jointly appearing offences) that are also known in the philosophy of action. In that tradition, with very few exceptions, there are hardly any studies on the structure of action written by legal philosophers.[6] Another noteworthy fact is that 'the criminal lawyers' theory of action' has been elaborated in complete independence from 'the philosophers' theory of action';[7] but this can perhaps be explained by the lack of studies (by legal philosophers) that could have served as a bridge between criminal lawyers and philosophers. In the Anglo-Saxon tradition, things were completely different, as the work of H. L. A. Hart,[8] Joel Feinberg,[9] or, to mention a more recent source, Michael S. Moore[10] on the philosophy of action and its applications in the criminal law testify. A telling evidence of the much stronger relation between philosophy and criminal law in the Anglo-Saxon world can be found in the assertion by George Fletcher, a criminal lawyer from the United States, that the criminal law is „a species of political and moral philosophy".[11] To Spanish ears, that is, to say the least, a very unusal opinion.

3. The book is structured as follows: In Chapter I, I summarily treat some prerequisites that need to be taken into account in an analysis of the concept of action. They are, basically, the problems posed by the 'language of action', the connexion between

[4] If only for this reason, a presentation of the main theories of action must contain a reference to the contributions of linguistic pragmatics.

[5] Austin 1979a, pp. 187 f. The relevance of the distinctions and the criteria established in the law for an investigation of the concept of action was already pointed out by Aristotle in the *Nicomachean Ethics*. For a summary of Aristotle's philosophy of action, cf. Rabossi 1997, pp. 5 ff.

[6] The most important exception is probably Carlos S. Nino (1972, 1980, 1987). A few other Spanish-speaking legal philosophers who have also given some thought to this topic are: Ricardo Guibourg 1987, Manuel Atienza 1984 (in this paper, a system of a logic of action developed by G. H. von Wright is adapted to some problems of criminal law), and Ernesto Garzón Valdés 1970 (containing a comparison of von Wright's and Hans Welzel's theories of action).

[7] A recent exception is Vives Antón 1996.

[8] Cf., above all, Hart 1949, 1973, and Hart/Honoré 1959.

[9] Feinberg 1968, 1988.

[10] Moore 1993.

[11] Quoted from Shute/Gardner/Horder 1993, p. 1.

actions and norms, and the problem of freedom and determinism. In Chapter II, I then formulate some more or less firm intuitions about the concept of action and try to show that they are mutually incompatible, giving rise to five paradoxes. In order to eliminate these paradoxes, we can, of course, simply assume that our intuitions are wrong; but before we draw that conclusion, we should at least analyze them in some detail. With the aim of finding a way out of the paradoxes, in Chapters III, IV, and V I review contributions to the theory of action from the philosophy of action, from criminal law, and from the philosophy of language (as already mentioned, I think that the paradoxes can be dissolved with the help of a distinction inspired, in turn, in Austin's distinction of the locutionary, the illocutionary, and the perlocutionary aspects of speech acts). In my view, a great many of the controversies among philosophers of action, on the one hand, and among lawyers, on the other, arise precisely because in each camp only one of these three aspects of action is considered. Such approaches lead to reductionist theories – focussing *either* on the natural aspect of actions, *or* on their subjective dimension, *or* on their social dimension – whereas the concept of action is actually much too complex to be reduced to one of its dimensions (this is perhaps the most important suggestion we owe to Austin, or at least one possible interpretation of his work). In Chapter VII, I then analyze the elements and the structure of action and try to present some conclusions of the preceding discussion in a clear and succinct way. Finally, Chapter VIII very briefly touches upon some questions concerning the distinction between natural and institutional actions and the concept of omission.

4. To conclude this preface, I wish to thank the members of the Department of Legal Philosophy at the University of Alicante for the discussions I have been privileged to have with them while writing this book, and for their many comments and suggestions. My very special thanks go to Manuel Atienza for his generous and perspicacious Foreword (he has put his finger precisely on some of my own deepest doubts about the concept of action), and to Ruth Zimmerling for the translation and her suggestions which helped me to recognize and correct a number of mistakes and confusions in the Spanish manuscript of this book.

CHAPTER I

PRELIMINARIES

1. The Concept of Action and the Traps of Language

Language sets us numerous little traps around the concept of action. We only need to look at ordinary language to become aware of some of them:

The first is hidden behind the fact that, except in evaluative contexts, the word 'action' is not used very frequently in ordinary language. This has already been pointed out, for instance, by John L. Austin,[1] and was noted also by Genaro Carrió who once wrote that „because of the vast arsenal of verbs we have at our disposition for isolating and characterizing different conducts, there is hardly any need to use the word 'action' in the ordinary language we use for all our practical purposes. That word, or the expression 'an action', only serves to isolate (but without characterizing) an instance of human behaviour, and it is not often the case that we need to do no more than that".[2] Does that mean that ordinary language cannot provide us with criteria for understanding the concept of action? If that is our conclusion, then I'm afraid we have already fallen into the first trap. Though it may be true that the term 'action' is not used very frequently in ordinary language, criteria for its application can nevertheless be found in it, because – as Nino has pointed out – the usual meaning of a word is determined not only by its actual usage, but also by people's willingness to accept or reject that usage when it does eventually occur. Thus, 'Today I did many things' may, however awkwardly, be replaced by 'Today I performed a great number of actions', whereas 'There were several giraffes in the zoo' obviously cannot be replaced by 'There were several actions in the zoo'.[3]

A second difficulty posed by ordinary language is the fact that the term 'action' is highly ambiguous and may adequately be used for referring to things which, despite having a certain 'family resemblance', are quite different: we speak of action as the production of a change in the world ('the action of closing the door'); of action as a disposition or character trait ('Alfred is a man of action'); of mental actions ('To think is a mental action'); of reflex action ('She was startled and hit him in a reflex action'); in the law, we also speak of 'action' as the possibility of bringing a claim to court; and we even use the word to encourage or give orders (as when a movie director shouts 'Action!'). Besides, we attribute action to the most diverse subjects: we say that Mary has performed a good action, that the action of storks is good for agriculture, that the action of the wind erodes the soil of the mountains, that the force of gravity is a kind of remote action, etc.

[1] Austin 1979a, pp. 178 ff.

[2] Carrió 1972, p. 11.

[3] Nino 1972, p. 137.

Another ambiguity of the term 'action' is that it can refer to a particular event that takes place at a specific time and place (such as the murder of Caesar by Brutus) as well as to a generic category of phenomena (such as the category of 'murder'). Action in the former sense is also called 'individual action', action in the latter sense is called 'generic action' or 'category of actions'.[4] The two senses are, of course, closely interrelated since every individual action belongs to some generic category of action.

Finally, a third problem is provoked by the fact that there are many partial synonyms of 'action' which together constitute a kind of conceptual family: 'act', 'activity', 'behaviour', and 'conduct' are a few of the more usual ones; but it is extremely difficult to formulate criteria for the correct use of each one of these synonyms.[5]

Because of the plurality of meanings of the word 'action', it is necessary to give a more precise account of the subject of this book. Unless otherwise indicated, I will refer exclusively to actions satisfying the following conditions:

(a) they are individual actions, that is, actions that take place at a specific time and in a specific place (though I will occasionally also have something to say about categories of actions);

(b) they are attributed to human beings;

(c) they are external (as opposed to mental actions), i. e., they include a bodily movement, however minimal it may be;

(d) they are positive, in the sense that by those bodily movements they produce some change;[6]

(e) they are voluntary (as opposed to reflex actions), i. e., there is some link between an agent's intention or will to produce a change and his bodily movements (regardless of what the content of that will or intention may be).

Some very relevant types of action are excluded by this choice, but it does encompass the most typical kinds. I think that this is an adequate strategy, because it enables me to construct a general scheme of the central cases of action, based on which one can then also study omissions, mental acts, reflex actions, etc., in terms of their greater or lesser compatibility with that scheme (that is what I will try to do in Chapter VIII, concerning the distinction between natural and institutional actions, and omissions). Besides, with this stipulation some difficulties can be avoided. But if we believe that we have there-

[4] Cf. von Wright 1963a, p. 36.

[5] With great caution, reservations and exceptions, one can perhaps say that, from the point of view of their structure, action and act are simpler than activity, conduct and behaviour: while the former can be understood as simple entities, the latter three seem to imply a sequence of acts or actions. From an evaluative point of view, on the other hand, action, act, activity, conduct, and behaviour can all appear in descriptive as well as in evaluative contexts: we speak of good actions, good acts, good conduct, unobjectionable behaviour, or valuable activities. In Nino's view, however, 'action' (when referring to human beings) is more frequently used in evaluative than in descriptive contexts. Nino suggests that this is so because the term 'action' underscores more than its partial synonyms the component of an agent's voluntariness; cf. Nino 1972, p. 136.

[6] I adopt the notion of change, or event, from von Wright, in the sense of a transition from one state of affairs to another, or to the same state of affairs. Cf. von Wright 1963a, p. 36.

fore already sailed around all the traps language has set us, we fall precisely into the most subtle of them all. In analyzing the debates that have taken place in the different disciplines over the concept of action, we will realize that they revolve around an ambiguity that is internal to the concept of action as it has just been traced, but which is due to a failure to distinguish three different aspects of actions.[7] That ambiguity I will call the 'deep ambiguity' of the term 'action'.

2. The Relevance of the Concept of Human Action for Ethics and the Law

The concept of action is an essential concept of law and ethics. Its relevance for both these fields is so great and obvious that it is difficult to give a precise description of it in a few lines, so I will only mention some aspects:

(a) First of all, the purpose of ethics and the law is to guide human action:

„To the extent that normative systems are schemes for the interpretation of behaviour and function as motives for the performance of desired, and the abstention from undesired, behaviour, action becomes the objective, and the description of action appears to be an indispensable basic resource for the integration of norms: hence, a theory of action is a necessary prerequisite for moral or legal philosophy.“[8]

Georg Henrik von Wright is one of the scholars who most firmly insist on the link between the concept of norm and the concept of action.[9] As he has shown, the content of a norm – that which is forbidden, obligatory or permitted – is always an action or a state of affairs that is brought about as the result of an action, and therefore a theory of action is, on that approach, a prerequisite for an adequate theory of norms.[10]

(b) If we focus our attention exclusively on ethics, we will find that this same author has distinguished three concepts that are of relevance in that field: normative concepts (such as 'obligation', 'permission', etc.), value-concepts ('good', 'bad', etc.), and concepts referring to human action ('act', 'desire', 'consequence', etc.).[11] The relation between the concept of action and ethics can then be seen as a triple connexion: *(i)* ethics must be directed towards the evaluation of persons and/or actions (where the criteria for the two things are not always the same); *(ii)* ethics (just as the law) presupposes that agents are, at least in some sense, free to act; and *(iii)* one of the most important distinctions between two of the most influential ethical conceptions – Kantian ethics and Benthamite utilitarianism (perhaps it is no exaggeration to say that they mark the extremes between which all other conceptions are located) – revolves around the

[7] Cf. Chapter VI.

[8] Guibourg 1987, p. 33.

[9] His most elaborate work on that topic is von Wright 1963a.

[10] Cf. von Wright 1968, p. 37 ff.

[11] Cf. von Wright 1963b, pp. 6 ff.

question which element of action (whether intention or consequences) is relevant, or more relevant, for their moral assessment.[12]

(c) If we now turn to the law, we only need to look at criminal and public law in order to comprehend the importance of the concept of action. In the criminal law, the concept of action has basically two functions: a 'negative' function and a 'coordinating' function. The negative function is that the notion of action allows a first delimitation of the sphere of crimes (or illicit acts in general): that which is not an action (in a broad sense which also includes omissions) cannot be a crime. We can see this immediately in the definition the continental theory of criminal law gives of an offence (an offence is a typified, unlawful and culpable *action*) and in what in Anglo-Saxon criminal law is known as the *actus reus* requirement. This is illustrated in the following formulation by P. J. Fitzgerald:

„The problem of defining an act owes its importance partly to the constant recurrence throughout the common law of a certain theme, namely the requirement of an act [...] In the Law of Torts we find that a man who has been carried bodily against his will onto the land of another has been held not liable in trespass because there was no act on his part, and in fact it has been suggested that in general a tort consists in some act done by the defendant whereby he has without just cause or excuse caused some form of harm to the plaintiff. But nowhere is this requirement so clearly seen as in the criminal law, where it manifests itself in the rule that *mens rea* by itself is not enough to constitute a crime: there must be an *actus reus*."[13]

But besides this negative function, the concept of action also has a positive, coordinating function in the criminal law. As Michael S. Moore remarks, the penal codes of all industrialized countries prohibit approximately 7.000 kinds of actions. In order to facilitate their application, these codes need some kind of structure. To give such structure to a code, one needs a concept of action that enables one to give generic answers (instead of having to give an answer for each one of the 7.000 types of prohibited actions) to the following questions: *(1)* What are the modes (consciously or unconsciously, by omission, etc.) in which an action can be performed?[14] *(2) Where* and *when* have the actions been performed? *(3)* What mental states are required for culpability? *(4)* In case one and the same action violates more than one prohibition, which punishment is to be applied? *(5)* How can one determine how many prohibited actions an agent has performed in a certain period of time?[15]

(d) In civil law, the concept of action also plays an important role. We can see this, for example, in the theory of legal facts and legal acts that has been developed in the civil-law doctrine (although it claims to be of a general nature and not limited to civil law).

[12] Thus, Martín D. Farrell (1983, p. 64) has remarked that „a coherent formulation of utilitarianism requires an adequate theory for the description of actions".

[13] Fitzgerald 1968, p. 120. On the interest of lawyers in the concept of action, cf. also Nino 1987, pp. 13-16.

[14] Occasionally, we must answer questions such as whether it is possible to kill by omission or while sleeping; but the answer we give for the case of 'killing' may not be valid for the case of 'robbing' because these are different types of actions. A concept of action must search for what the two types of actions have in common and must offer generic answers to the question.

[15] Cf. Moore 1993, pp. 1 ff.

The dominant doctrine defines legal facts in a broad sense as „those events or situations that are of importance in the life of the law because they have been stipulated by a norm as a factor which determines some legal consequence".[16] Legal facts in that broad sense comprise „natural legal facts" and „human legal facts". The former are those that occur independently of human action (such as earthquakes, floods, or the passage of time). The latter, in contrast, are the result of human conducts. Within this group, lawyers distinguish between „legal facts in the strict sense" and „legal acts". The difference between them is that for the former, the consequence stipulated in the norm is produced regardless of whether or not the agent intends to bring about that consequence, whereas the latter produce legal consequences only if the agent had the intention of bringing them about. Thus, for example, unlawful acts are legal facts in the strict sense, since their legal consequences come about regardless of whether or not the agent had the intention of triggering them (moreover, in that case it is usually assumed that there was no such intention); in contrast, to make a will is a legal act (or, as lawyers also say, a declaration of will) since it has an effect only if the agent had the intention of making a will.[17] Obviously, these distinctions in civil law turn on the notions of action and intention.

(e) The considerations of the criminal law show a new type of link between norms and actions: Not only are actions part of the content of norms; precisely because of they are, norms in turn become a scheme of interpretation for certain kinds of actions (thus, for example, what makes us distinguish between 'killing' and 'murdering' is that we interpret the latter in terms of a certain norm).

(f) The distinctions drawn in the civil law go even further and show that some actions (those civil lawyers call 'legal acts') are not only interpreted in the light of norms: they can only be performed if the agent makes use of the norms which indicate to him what he must do in order to perform them (here, I am referring to norms that confer public or private powers, or competence norms, i. e., norms that stipulate the conditions for making a valid will, pronouncing a sentence, passing a law, etc.).

In most philosophical theories of action, the perspectives for the concept of action which open up if one takes into account these links between norms and actions have been neglected; but it may be useful to pay closer attention to them.

3. Human Freedom as a Prerequisite

Although I will treat our intuitions about action in the next chapter, there is one initial intuition that is a prerequisite for any theory of action. This intuition, which is reflected in ordinary language, establishes – so firmly that in my view all argument to the contrary is useless – that at least sometimes (which is sufficient) people act freely. This means that on some occasions, when a person has acted in a certain way she could also

[16] Cf. Puig Brutau 1950-1993 p. 836.

[17] Cf. Aguiló Regla 2000.

have chosen to act differently, or not to act at all. This conviction is the very foundation for the distinction between the actions we perform and the things that happen to us, between our condition of acting subjects and our condition of passive sufferers. Against the arguments of determinists, we can say the same thing Hume said against the arguments of Berkeley: „*they admit of no answer and produce no conviction*“.[18]

Peter F. Strawson has given an elaborate account of that opinion, starting from our basic social intuitions and attitudes. Strawson describes a kind of attitude we display in our social relationships (and which he considers an essential component of them). This attitude, which he calls a 'reactive attitude', consists of a reaction (gratitude, resentment, forgiveness, love, hurt feelings, etc.) to the attitudes with which others perform actions that affect us. For example, if someone gives us a shove, our reactions will be very different, depending on whether we think that it happened by accident or intentionally. If we believe in an accident, we will be more willing to forgive the other, or will not even be offended at all. If we believe in an intention, we will probably be less forgiving and more offended. Sometimes, we suspend our reactive attitudes and replace them by what Strawson calls an 'objective attitude', for example when we are dealing with the actions of a lunatic or of someone who has been physically pushed to do something without being able to avoid it. The objective attitude implies that we suspend our indignation, resentment, gratitude, etc. Now, if determinism were true, would this imply that the objective attitude would be extended to all interpersonal relationships? Strawson thinks that it is unlikely that a theoretical belief might change our social foundations in such a radical way, and he even asserts that this is not a matter we could rationally decide since it touches on an aspect of our life that is so basic and fundamental that it is beyond our criteria of rationality.[19] As Nino has remarked, the same reasoning would apply if one started from many other fundamental practices and institutions of social life, such as, for instance, consensus or legal and moral responsibility.[20]

[18] Hume 1975 (1777), Sect. 122, n.

[19] Strawson 1974.

[20] Nino 1987, p. 107.

CHAPTER II

OUR INTUITIONS AND THE PARADOXES OF ACTION

1. Introduction

When we undertake an analysis of the concept of action, we can immediately come up with a number of assertions which seem plausible enough to serve as a starting point for a theory of action. As long as we look at them one at a time, they appear to be intuitive theses that can easily be inferred from an analysis of ordinary language. Thus, they seem to express more or less firmly established truths. Unfortunately, however, these theses confront us with a great inconvenience: they are not easily compatible with each other. Take the following ten assertions:[1]

> *(1) Actions are a kind of events that occur in the physical world and have an 'impact' on it.*
>
> *(2) Actions have preferable descriptions.*
> When I perform an action, I bring about many changes that are irrelevant for the description of my action; for instance, if I take a walk in the park I also move molecules in the air, wear down the soles of my shoes, and change my position relative to the North Pole; but descriptions in terms of these changes are not – normally – relevant for the identification of my action.
>
> *(3) Actions (at least, many actions) are identified by bodily movements.*
> This is an intuitive assertion which is said to be based on „two basic commonsense propositions", to wit: *(a)* that we no longer act when we are dead, and *(b)* that at least some actions (such as taking a walk through the park or smoking) can be seen by others.[2]
>
> *(4) One and the same bodily movement can, depending on circumstances, give rise to different actions.*
> Thus, for example, the lifting of an arm may be an action of greeting, threatening, calling for help, etc.; the same movement may constitute a dance, an exercise, a signal, etc.
>
> *(5) Instances of one and the same generic action or act-category can be performed through different bodily movements.*

[1] Some of them have been formulated in Searle 1984, ch. 4.

[2] Cf. Nino 1987, p. 23.

For example, the action of sending a message to a friend may be performed by writing a letter, making a phone call, sending a telegram, and so on; a person may be killed by a gunshot, by strangulation, by poisoning, by stabbing, etc.

(6) People have privileged knowledge about the actions they themselves perform.
We do not need to observe ourselves or conduct an investigation in order to find out what actions we perform. Knowledge about the action we are performing at any point in time does not depend on the observation of our own bodily movements – in contrast to the knowledge others can have about our actions. Even if I perform a sequence of bodily movements that can be interpreted as two or more different actions, I myself will have no doubt about which one of these I am performing. As Hampshire and Hart have pointed out, there is something wrong with the question 'How do you know that you are doing *x*?'.[3]

(7) Under normal conditions, it is not difficult for us to know what actions others are performing.
We are used to interpreting the movements of others in terms of what it is they are doing, what their purpose is, why they are making those movements. In performing such interpretations, we apply certain principles and criteria that we have learned. But we are conscious of that process only in some cases in which it is not obvious what the person we are observing actually means to be doing; in most cases, we are not aware of the process of identifying actions, we do it unconsciously.

(8) We attribute actions to others regardless of their own criteria, and make them responsible for them.
We do this in accordance with the principles and criteria mentioned in the previous point. That is what blaming others and making them liable for their negligent actions is based on.

(9) To perform an action is to produce a change in the world.
This is one of the most common approaches to the concept of action because one of the surest ways of examining whether or not a certain action has been successfully performed is to check whether the change in the world intended by the agent has in fact taken place (and whether there is some relation between the agent's movements and that change).

(10) Often (perhaps always) our actions have more than one consequence, and we cannot foresee them all.

If we examine these ten theses in conjunction, we will find that they contain several paradoxes or inconsistencies.

[3] Cf. Hampshire/Hart 1958, p. 8.

2. First Paradox: Are Actions Natural Phenomena or Products of Our Worldview?

The first inconsistency already arises between assertions *(1)* and *(2)*. According to thesis *(1)*, actions belong to the physical, empirical world: they are observable phenomena which exist in the same way as physical objects or natural events. Actions hence constitute what some philosophers have called a 'natural class' (i. e., they exist independently of rules and conventions, although our understanding of them may be informed by conventional elements). Assertion *(2)*, in contrast, has given rise to theories that tend to locate actions outside of the physical world, converting them into little more than a peculiarity of language or of our interpretation of the world (an idea that becomes more evident in the case of omissions). According to this thesis, the specific characteristic of actions is not something in the physical world, but something in the language with which we describe the physical world, and in the ideas we project onto it. In that direction, we can find more or less radical positions. Michael S. Moore refers to some of the more radical ones as 'skeptical theories' because they deny that actions exist (or at least, that they exist as natural phenomena). Moore includes in this group the ascriptive theory of Hart who in his 'The Ascription of Responsibility and Rights' said (although he later retracted it) that sentences about actions do not describe anything at all, that they have no reference, and that they rather fulfil another linguistic function, namely, that of ascribing responsibility to an agent.[4] One could also regard as skeptical the theories of authors who adopt what Moore calls an 'interpretative attitude'. This is the case, for example, of George Fletcher and Mark Kelman, or of philosophers such as Daniel Dennett for whom the difference between an action and something that is not an action is determined exclusively by the interpretation an observer gives to an event from a teleological or intentional point of view. For these authors, actions are actions only because we interpret them as such; but we could perfectly well also adopt another point of view from which we would see no difference between actions and other natural events (for example, from a deterministic point of view, we would see them entangled in a web of causes and effects).[5]

3. Second Paradox: : Are Actions Bodily Movements or Descriptions of Bodily Movements?

More problems, related to the previous one,[6] arise when we compare assertions *(3)*, *(4)* and *(5)*. According to assertion *(3)*, it seems plausible to analyze actions as bodily movements; but assertions *(4)* and *(5)* show that there is no one-to-one correspondence between kinds of actions and bodily movements. From the fact that one and the same

[4] Hart 1949; for a summary of this theory, cf. below Chapter III, sect. 3.

[5] Moore 1993, pp. 9, 61-65.

[6] However, the problems are not identical, because one could hold that actions are 'natural classes' and still deny that they are bodily movements (for example, some authors prefer to identify them with mental states, such as 'volitions').

action can be performed through different bodily movements, and that one and the same bodily movement can, depending on circumstances, constitute different actions, many authors (e. g., A. I. Melden and R. Peters) draw the conclusion that actions cannot be identified with bodily movements.[7] Moreover, against such an identification other arguments have been brought forward, such as the one saying that actions are usually described in terms of the circumstances and consequences of such bodily movements and not exclusively mentioning the movements themselves. But, on the other hand, if we were to renounce linking actions with bodily movements, we would lose one of our most solid supports for any theory of action that presents action as a natural phenomenon, and also the possibility to distinguish between actions, such as running, killing, closing a door, and things like calculating, praying, remembering, etc., which we would be willing to call 'actions' only in a secondary sense (expressed through the attribute 'mental').

4. Third Paradox: Can We Be Mistaken About Our Own Actions?

The third inconsistency we encounter when we consider assertions *(6)*, *(7)*, and *(8)*. Assertion *(6)* must be linked to the notion of intention – a notion many authors have understood in the sense of a mental state that (in some sense) causes the action and at the same time serves to identify it. Understood in this way, a person's intentions are regarded as a mental state (just like pain or sadness) that is specificly related to that person, in a way philosophers designate with words such as 'subjectivity', 'introspection', 'privileged access', etc. If intention is an essential constitutive element of actions and agents have special (and, under normal conditions, infallible) access to their own actions, then there is a sense in which agents cannot be mistaken about the actions they themselves perform. Sentences about actions in the first person have a special status because agents have knowledge about their own actions that is not the result of an inference or observation.

But, does it follow from this that an agent has the *only* say about his own actions? Assertion *(7)* clearly denies this: despite that internal nature of intention which supposedly makes access for others difficult, our experience shows that very often we are not mistaken in attributing actions to others. Although our knowledge about the actions of others is indirect and requires observation and interpretation of their bodily movements, apart from cases that seem to be exceptional we usually take it to be sufficiently reliable. So can we say at least that agents have the *last word* about their own actions? Again, it seems that this is not the case, because if assertion *(8)* is true, then we attribute actions to agents even regardless of their own criteria (and despite the fact that we admit that our knowledge about the actions of others is less reliable than their own knowledge about them). Does that mean, then, that we can be mistaken after all when we say which actions we have or have not performed ourselves?

This question needs qualification. There are several senses in which an agent can be said to be mistaken about his own actions: *(i)* he may wish to do one thing, but

[7] Cf. Moore 1993, p. 90.

actually do another (e. g., he may wish to turn on the warm water, but actually turn on the cold); *(ii)* he may mistakenly believe to have performed a certain action which he actually did not perform because the corresponding result did not come about (e. g., he may believe to have killed someone who actually was only injured); *(iii)* he may choose a wrong course of action, that is, one that is not adequate for his purpose (a favourite example of lawyers is that of the person who tries to poison another with sugar in the belief that it is a powerful poison); *(iv)* he may perform certain bodily movements that may be described as a number of different actions (when someone lifts his arm, we may not be able to tell whether he is greeting a friend, calling for help, signaling a danger, threatening someone, etc.). In the last case, when there are several possible descriptions of the same bodily movements, it would, however, be strange – and even paradoxical – to say that there was a mistake in the action.

5. Fourth Paradox: Do We Perform Several Actions With One Single Bodily Movement? (The 'Accordion Effect' of Actions)

Assertions *(9)* and *(10)* point to a characteristic that is frequently attributed to actions. Joel Feinberg has called it the 'accordion effect'. When we act, we do this in order to bring about a change in the world that for some reason we desire. If acting is bringing about or (in a broad sense) causing a change, it seems that propositions of the type '*A* caused the door to close' are equivalent to propositions of the kind '*A* closed the door'. The difficulties begin when we recognize that the change we have brought about can be the cause of another change, and that one of yet another, and so on, in a chain of causes and effects triggered by our initial bodily movement. This leads to a peculiar feature of actions, or at least of their descriptions. In Feinberg's words:

„This well-known feature of our language, whereby a man's action can be described as narrowly or broadly as we please, I propose to call the 'accordion effect', because an act, like the folding musical instrument, can be squeezad down to a minimum or else stretched out. He turned the key, he opened the door, he startled Smith, he killed Smith – all of these are things we might say that Jones did with one identical set of bodily movements."[8]

The 'accordion effect' of actions leads to two paradoxes. The first is the following: Can different consequences of the same bodily movements constitute different actions? If I make certain bodily movements which produce several consequences, have I performed several actions with the same movements?

An example quoted by Nino illustrates the importance of that paradox for the criminal law (which treats that problem under the somewhat broader heading of 'offences committed jointly'):

„Some beggars mutilate children in order to be more successful with their collection of alms; some of them die as a consequence of the injuries. Obviously, although they accepted the risk of that result, the beggars did not mutilate *in order to* kill, since the children's death was actually incompatible with their purposes. The

[8] Feinberg 1968, p. 106.

question it is reasonable to ask then is: did the beggars perform two actions, that of mutilating and that of killing, or only one which, of course, permits two alternative descriptions?“[9]

6. Fifth Paradox: What Are the Limits of Our Actions?

The second paradox in relation with the ‘accordion effect’ concerns the question which consequences of my bodily movements are to be considered actions: All of them? Or perhaps only the consequences most closely linked to the movements? In other words: How far are we willing to take the equivalence of propositions about actions and propositions about the production of changes?

Suppose, for example, Alfred invites his aunt Adela to his home for lunch, and during that lunch he opens the window, which causes a draught that affects Aunt Adela’s delicate health, leading to her death. With a minimal theory of causality (i. e., a theory saying only that a cause is any condition about which one can say that, had it not occurred, the consequence would not have been produced), we can say that Alfred *caused the death* of his aunt. But would we be willing to say that Alfred *killed* Aunt Adela? Note that this is actually not a question about where the chain of causes and effects initiated with Alfred’s bodily movements ends, because I may well admit that those movements were the remote cause of Aunt Adela’s death and still deny that Alfred has performed the action of killing her, i. e., deny that consequence the *status of an action.*

There are good reasons for limiting our notion of action, but it is not easy to propose a well-founded criterion for such limitation. Some authors – among them, for instance, Michael S. Moore – therefore argue that the only limits we have are those stipulated by the idiomatic usage of each verb of action, and that, strictly speaking, the two kinds of propositions – those in terms of actions and those in terms of the production of effects – are always equivalent.[10]

The paradoxical nature of all these questions derives from the fact that there seem to be good reasons, of more or less equal weight, for each and every possible answer to each one of them. Many theories of action have rejected (if not explicitly, then at least implicitly, as a consequence of their assumptions) one or the other of the theses I have presented, in order to avoid the inconsistencies implied in their joint admission. I will go the opposite way, taking the theses for granted and exploring the idea that the inconsistencies between them are only apparent, due to the ‘internal’ or ‘deep’ ambiguity of the term ‘action’. In order to account for that ambiguity and to find the tools with which we can dissolve it, we must now review the most relevant theories of action elaborated in the philosophy of action, in criminal-law doctrine, and in the philosophy of language, respectively.

[9] Nino 1972, p. 43.

[10] Cf. Moore 1993, p. 237.

CHAPTER III

THE DEBATE IN THE PHILOSOPHY OF ACTION

1. The Controversy About the Individuation of Actions

Around the beginning of the '60s, studies about the concept of action and related notions such as intention, motive, reason, etc., proliferated and became an important focus of philosophical debate, especially among philosophers of an analytical orientation. It would probably be wrong to say that there was only one single reason for this development; but the discussion about the proper method of the human sciences is usually mentioned as one of the most important reasons. For Richard Bernstein, for instance, the interest in the philosophy of action grew with the reaction within analytical philosophy itself against the reductionism of authors such as Carnap or the early Wittgenstein. That reaction manifested itself in the form of a 'new teleology', emphasizing the intentional, purposive nature of human actions.[1]

The debate I am interested in here, however, is not – or not directly – that about the relationship between intention and action, or about the most adequate method for the human sciences (the subject of which, in the last instance, is human action), although it may be regarded as an offspring of these. Basically, I will consider what has been known as the controversy about the individuation of actions, because I think that it is focused more directly on the concept of action itself.

The issues that were at stake in that controversy can be presented with the help of a historical example. In 1914, in Sarajevo, Gavrilo Princip shot and killed the Archduke Francis Ferdinand. The sequence of Princip's actions can be described as follows: he drew his pistol, put his right forefinger around the trigger, aimed the weapon at the Archduke, bent his right forefinger, pulled the trigger, fired the pistol, hit the Archduke with the bullit, wounded the Archduke, and killed the Archduke. Do all these descriptions of what Princip did refer to different actions? The answer depends on our position concerning the individuation of actions. If I say that Princip did all these things, then I am saying that by simply moving his fingers he has carried out several actions (among them, those of moving his fingers, pulling the trigger, firing the pistol, and killing the Archduke). Others perhaps prefer to say that Princip performed only one action, namely, that of moving his fingers, by which he caused the Archduke's death (and, perhaps, the First World War).

Let us look at a more simple example: I walk along the street and see a friend approaching from the opposite direction, so I think I should greet him and lift my arm as a greeting. In lifting my arm to greet my friend, have I performed a single action, or two actions (that of lifting the arm *and* that of greeting)? The question is easily stated, but not quite as easily answered, and the problem of the individuation of actions (i. e., the

[1] Cf. Bernstein 1971, ch. 4.

problem of answering questions like the one above) has given rise, as already mentioned, to a heated controversy among philosophers of action. The main protagonists of that debate have been Donald Davidson and Alvin I. Goldman. They have adopted radically different standpoints. While Davidson's position has been called, in a certain sense, 'minimizing' (for him, in cases like that of Princip there is only one single action), Goldman's position is 'maximizing' (for Goldman, there are as many actions as there are possible descriptions).[2]

1. THE MINIMIZING POSITION

1.1. Davidson's position (which I take from G. E. M. Anscombe)[3] starts from what Joel Feinberg calls the 'accordion effect' of actions (which was already mentioned in Chapter II). According to Feinberg, all the things we do with one and the same bodily movement are different actions. In our example, that means that moving one's fingers and killing someone would be different actions, with different effects (namely, that Princip's fingers have been moved, and that the Archduke has been killed). Now, as Davidson points out, these actions happen at different moments in time and should be causally related. That should lead us to consider that Princip's action of moving his fingers caused his action of pulling the trigger, and that this caused his action of firing the gun, which, in turn, caused the action of shooting the Archduke, which caused the action of killing the Archduke, which was the action that caused the death of the Archduke. This characterization of events seems rather complicated (it requires the introduction of the idea of causation between actions, perhaps as a special type of causal relationships), especially if we take into consideration that moving one's fingers in a certain manner in the context of the example is sufficient for the Archduke to die, without any need that it should cause the action of killing him, or any of the other, intermediate actions. Therefore, Davidson says:

„[T]his welter of related descriptions corresponds to a single *descriptum* [...] When we infer that he stopped his car from the fact that by pressing a pedal a man caused his automobile to come to a stop, we do not transfer agency from one event to another, or infer that the man was agent not only of one action but of two. We may indeed extend responsibility or liability for an action to responsibility or liability for its consequences, but this we do, not by saddling the agent with a new action, but by pointing out that his original action had those results."[4]

[2] Cf. Ginet 1990, p. 47. Between these extreme positions, we find authors who advocate intermediate criteria for the individuation of actions, i. e., they hold what can perhaps be called 'moderate maximizing' positions.

[3] The problem of the individuation of actions was presented by Elizabeth Anscombe in her book *Intention* with the following question: „Are we to say that the man who (intentionally) moves his arm, operates the pump, replenishes the water supply, poisons the inhabitants, is performing *four* actions? Or only one?" And she answers that question thus: „In short, the only distinct action of his that is in question is this one, A. For moving his arm up and down with his fingers round the punp handle *is*, in these circumstances, operating the pump; and, in these circumstances, it *is* replenishing the house water-supply; and, in these circumstances, it *is* poisoning the household." (Anscombe 1963, § 26, pp. 45, 46)

[4] Davidson 1980, p. 59.

From this, Davidson concludes that „mere movements of the body [...] are all the actions there are“ and that „we never do more than move our bodies: the rest is up to nature“.[5]
The following table sums up Anscombe's and Davidson's opinion on this issue:[6]

DESCRIPTIONS

Princip moves his fingers		Princip pulls the trigger		Princip shoots at the Archduke		Princip kills the Archduke
↑		↑		↑		↑
Princip's fingers move	→	The trigger moves	→	The pistol goes off	→	The Archduke dies

EVENTS

Here, '→' designates a causal relationship between events, and '↑' can be read as 'generates the description'. The accordion effect is explained by observing that a bodily movement gives rise to a chain of events each of which allows a new description of the same action (that is, the accordion effect does not affect the actions themselves, but only the descriptions of actions). This position, however, does not imply any kind of reductionism, because neither Davidson nor the other advocates of this thesis claim that the description of an action in terms of bodily movements (or any other particular kind of description) is preferable or 'more closely' linked to the action; after all, we can also give different descriptions, for example, of a table, without having to commit ourselves to any one of these descriptions in particular.

1.2. The minimizing theory has the merit of clarity (from this perspective, 'counting actions' seems to be an easy task, although this is true only in principle because the problem of delimiting the sequence of bodily movements which constitute an action remains), but this comes at the cost of several inconveniences. As we will see in the next section, Goldman has serious objections against the thesis of identity. To these, we must also add that it is inconsistent with our linguistic habits (which might be an indicator of

5 Ibid.

6 The table is adapted from Moya 1990, p. 31.

a more profound problem) concerning responsibility and the distinction between intentional and non-intentional actions.

We have seen that as one way of solving the problems of individuation Davidson proposes that we should „try talking not of actions but of sentences and descriptions of actions instead“[7]; but that may suppose an excessive reformulation of ordinary language. First of all, in ordinary language (and in the language of ethics and the law), we are willing to accept sentences like the following: 'Princip is responsible for having performed the action of killing the Archduke' (or 'Princip is responsible for having killed the Archduke'). But in order to be consistent with Davidson's theory, we would have to say that 'Princip is responsible for having performed an action that can be described as »having killed the Archduke«', which seems a strange way of speaking. Secondly (and this is a more important objection), according to the thesis of identity, the distinction between intentional and non-intentional actions would be only a distinction between two types of descriptions. In fact, Davidson and Anscombe say that an action may be intentional under one description, but not under another. Davidson gives the following example: Hamlet had the intention of killing the man behind the arras, who happened to be Polonius. What Hamlet did can be described as *(1)* 'He killed the man behind the arras' and as *(2)* 'He killed Polonius'. 'Under description (1)', Hamlet's action was intentional, 'under description (2)', it was not.[8] But the distinction between intentional and non-intentional actions is such a deep-rooted intuition that it seems to be more than just a peculiarity of our language. As Searle remarked, what matters in that distinction is not how we describe an action, but „what these descriptions are actually describing“.[9]

These problems can be solved with a criterion for the individuation of actions as that proposed by Alvin I. Goldman.

2. THE MAXIMIZING POSITION

2.1. In *A Theory of Human Action* (1976) and 'The Individuation of Action' (1971), Goldman criticized with several arguments what he calls Anscombe's and Davidson's 'identity thesis'. For Goldman, their position amounts to the claim that in examples as that of Princip, 'moving one's finger' is the same as 'pulling the trigger', which is the same as 'firing the weapon', which is the same as 'killing the Archduke'. Generally, for the identity thesis the different descriptions of an action refer to identical events, and that means: to one and the same event.[10] Now, if that were indeed the case, then serious objections could be raised:

(a) The first objection is that this identification would violate Leibniz's principle according to which, if any two things x and y are identical, then every property of x is

[7] Davidson 1980a, p. 46.

[8] This characterization of intentional actions is related to the phenomenon linguists call 'reference opacity'. On this, cf. below, Chapter VII, sect. 6.2.

[9] Searle 1983, p. 92.

[10] Goldman 1971, p. 762.

also a property of *y*. In many cases in which the identity thesis sees one single action, that principle is not satisfied with respect to the causes, effects and evaluative properties. For example, the action of saying 'Hello' and the action of saying 'Hello' in a dry tone at one and the same time *t* have different causes (the action of 'saying Hello at time *t*' has as its cause the wish to greet someone, and the action of 'saying Hello in a dry tone at time *t*' has as its cause some resentment in the agent), although Davidson or Anscombe would say that it is one and the same action.[11] The action of moving one's fingers has another effect as the action of killing someone (that the fingers move in the former, and that someone dies in the latter case), although again the identity thesis would imply that it is one and the same action. Finally, when we pay a debt to a friend at time *T*, we perform an obligatory action; but when we pay the debt at the same time *T* with a bill we know he would like to have in his collection, we perform an act of courtesy. Once more, the evaluative properties of the two actions are different, although for the criticized conception we are dealing with one single action.

(b) Another objection Goldman raises against the identity thesis is based on the kind of mutual relationship between actions like those in the previous examples. Thus, we say that Princip killed the Archduke *by* firing the pistol, that he fired the pistol *by* pulling the trigger, and that he pulled the trigger *by* moving his finger. Goldman notes that this ordering is not arbitrary: it shows that the relationship between these descriptions is one of means and ends, not of iguality. Thus, while we say that Princip killed the Archduke *by* firing the gun, we cannot say with the same sense that he fired his gun *by* killing the Archduke.[12]

(c) Finally, the identity thesis blurs the distinction (which seems intuitively plausible to Goldman and which is widely accepted among philosophers) between basic actions and other actions. If performing an action a_1 is done *by* performing another action a_2, and this in turn is done *by* performing an action a_3, and so on, then if we want to avoid an infinite regress, at some point the process must stop. And it stops precisely with basic[13] or simple[14] actions, which are actions we perform directly, and not through other actions. Most (but not all)[15] authors identify basic actions with bodily movements, that is, precisely with the only kind of actions that exist according to Davidson and Anscombe.

Goldman proposes as a solution to these problems a criterion of individuation that starts from a distinction between what he calls 'act-types' (or 'act-properties') and 'act-tokens".[16] Act-types are a kind of properties:

[11] For Goldman, in contrast, they are two different actions.

[12] At least in Spanish, the latter formulation also makes sense, but only in the first case are we referring to a means-ends relationship.

[13] Cf. Danto 1968, p. 44.

[14] Feinberg 1968, p. 107.

[15] Hugh McCann, for example, identifies basic actions with our volitions. On basic actions, cf., e. g., Moya 1990, chs. 1 and 2.

[16] Goldman's distinction is very similar to the one von Wright draws between generic and individual actions. For von Wright, a generic action is a category of actions defined by some property. An individual action is a

„An act type, as I construe it, is simply an act property, something that an agent exemplifies. When we say 'John weighed 170 pounds' or 'John was bald', we ascribe to John the property of weighing 170 pounds or the property of being bald. Similarly, I suggest that when we say 'John signaled for a turn' or 'John killed George', we ascribe act properties or act types to John: the property of signaling for a turn or the property of killing George."[17]

An act-token or particular act is the exemplification of an act-type by a particular agent at a particular point in time:
„To perform an act, then, is to exemplify a property. To perform the act of giving a lecture is to exemplify the property of giving a lecture. A particular act, then, consists in the exemplifying of an act-property by an agent at a particular time. I shall call such particular acts: 'act-tokens'. An act-token is not itself a property. It is the exemplifying of a property by an agent."[18]

With these precisions, Goldman says that two actions are identical if and only if they refer to the same agent, the same property and the same time. If we now apply this criterion to the example of Princip, moving his fingers, pulling the trigger, firing the arm, and killing the Archduke are different actions, because each one exemplifies another property. But although they may be different actions, there is nevertheless a certain relationship between them. According to Goldman, between the actions produced by one and the same basic action (which gives rise to an 'act-tree'), there are generational relations. These can be of different kinds:

(1) of *causal generation*, when the relationship between the actions depends on relationships of causality;

(2) of *conventional generation*, when an action performed in certain circumstances produces another action because there is a rule to that effect (for example, when a chess player moves the queen to a certain field and thereby obtains a checkmate);

(3) of *simple generation*, when an action is a sufficient condition for the production of another, but it is neither a case of causal nor of conventional generation (for example, the relationship between jumping *x* meters and jumping farther than anyone else in history);

(4) of *augmentation generation*, when the first action is augmented by additional circumstances and facts, and – in contrast to what happens in simple generation – there is no relationship of implication (for example, 'saying Hello' and 'saying Hello in a loud voice' at the same time).[19]

Goldman's thesis can be represented in the following table, where '→' designates a causal generation between actions, '➥' a relationship of causality between an action

particular instance of an action which has the property of some generic action. This distinction appears in many of his works, but it is most extensively treated in von Wright 1983, pp. 112 ff.

[17] Goldman 1971, p. 769.

[18] Goldman 1976, p. 10.

[19] Goldman 1976, Sect. i ('Level-Generation'), pp. 20 ff.

and an event, '↕ ' the relationship between an action and an event that must hold so that we can say that the action has been performed, and '↑' the relation of exemplification:

<table>
<tr><td>Moving one's fingers</td><td></td><td>Pulling a trigger</td><td></td><td>Firing</td><td></td><td>Killing</td><td>ACT-TYPES</td></tr>
<tr><td>↑</td><td></td><td>↑</td><td></td><td>↑</td><td></td><td>↑</td><td></td></tr>
<tr><td>Princip moves his fingers</td><td>→</td><td>Princip pulls the trigger</td><td>→</td><td>Princip fires</td><td>→</td><td>Princip kills the Archduke</td><td>ACT-TOKENS</td></tr>
<tr><td>|</td><td></td><td>↕ |</td><td></td><td>↕ |</td><td></td><td>↕</td><td></td></tr>
<tr><td>➥</td><td>The trigger moves</td><td>➥</td><td>The arm goes off</td><td>➥</td><td>The Arch-duke dies</td><td></td><td>EFFECTS</td></tr>
</table>

Princip moves his fingers (basic action), thereby exemplifying the property of moving one's fingers; his action causes the trigger of the gun he holds in his hand to move; this permits us to say that Princip has pulled the trigger and that there is a relationship of (in this case, causal) generation between the basic action and the action 'Princip pulls the trigger', which in turn is an exemplification of the property 'pulling a trigger' and causes the event 'the fire-arm goes off', which in its turn allows us to say that Princip has fired, which in turn ..., and so on. Has this not become just a bit too complicated?

2.2. One of the criticisms Goldman has objected against is that he introduces too many entities (act-tokens, act-properties, basic acts, and act-trees) whereas Davidson explains practically the same thing at lower ontological costs (he speaks only of basic acts and descriptions of acts). But that is only a first impression. If we analyze the positions of the advocates of the identity thesis and of the 'multipliers', we find that they are neither very far apart nor are their ontological requirements very different. In the following table, the notions used by Davidson and Goldman are compared:

Davidson	*Goldman*
Action	Basic Action
Description of an action	Action
Set of descriptions of an action	Act-Tree

In fact, the debate between maximizers and minimizers seems to be merely a verbal disagreement, as Héctor Neri Castañeda,[20] Carl Ginet,[21] and Carlos S. Nino,[22] among others, have remarked.

A more serious objection against Goldman's 'maximizing' position is the following: In his view, there are as many actions (i. e., act-tokens) as there are act-properties exemplified by an agent at a certain time. The consequence of this is that the number of actions an agent can simultaneously perform at one moment in time is impossible to count since one can exemplify an indeterminate number of act-properties at any time.[23] Goldman (who holds that a theory of the individuation of actions need not offer a criterion for counting actions)[24] accepts that consequence, but to many authors it may seem inacceptable. Besides, Goldman's criterion of individuation permits one to say that 'to say Hello at time *t*' and 'to say Hello in a dry tone at time *t*' are two different actions (which is hardly intuitively plausible) because he thinks that 'to say Hello' and 'to say Hello in a dry tone' are different properties (Goldman assumes that two properties are equal if and only if they are analytically equivalent).[25] Finally, Goldman has difficulties – as he himself admits – to offer a criterion for the distinction between those properties exemplified by an agent that are not linked to any action (such as being tall or bald) and those he calls 'act-properties'.[26]

One way to avoid the excessive multiplication of actions without adopting Davidson's theory consists in trying to offer criteria for distinguishing those properties that do and those that do not permit the individuation of an action. In that way, an action still is the exemplification of a property – that is, a case of some class of actions –, but not of any kind of property, and not even of any of the properties Goldman would consider an 'act-property'. There are, in fact, two theories that can be *reinterpreted* as proposals of criteria for choosing which properties among all those exemplified by a sequence of bodily movements or by an agent permit the individuation of actions: one of them is von Wright's distinction between a result and a consequence; the other is Hart's ascriptivist theory of action.[27]

2. Individuation From the Agent's Point of View (G. H. von Wright)

[20] Castañeda 1979; I owe this reference to Nino 1987, p. 51.

[21] Ginet 1990, p. 70.

[22] Nino 1987, p. 52.

[23] Goldman 1971, p. 772.

[24] Ibid., p. 773.

[25] Ginet 1990, p. 48.

[26] Goldman 1976, pp. 15 ff.

[27] Von Wright's and Hart's theses were not originally meant to intervene in that debate; but they can easily be reinterpreted in the light of it.

One of von Wright's most illuminating contributions to the theory of action is the distinction between a result and a consequence. For von Wright an action is the intentional production of a change in the world, and he defines changes or events as „the transition from one state of affairs to another".[28] Hence, a description of an action in terms of states of affairs must state *(a)* the state of affairs in the world at the beginning of the action (initial state), *(b)* the state of affairs in the world when the action has been completed (end-state), and *(c)* the state of affairs „in which the world would be had the agent not interfered with it".[29] The end-state (or the change concluding in that state) is what von Wright calls the 'result' of the action. In his theory of action, results play a very important role:

„By the *result* of an act we can understand either the change corresponding to this act or, alternatively, the end-state [...] of this change. Thus, by the result of the act of opening a certain window we can understand either the fact that the window is opening (changes from closed to open) or the fact that it is open."[30]

There are three aspects of this notion that deserve to be taken into consideration:

(1) The relationship between an action and its result (i. e., the change that has taken place or its end-state) is a logical or conceptual relationship. That means that if the final state of affairs does not come about, then the action has not taken place, and an individual action cannot be described as an act of a particular category if the end-state corresponding to the respective category of actions is not produced.

(2) The result of an action may give rise to further transformations in the world, with which it is then causally related. Changes that are causally produced by the result of an action von Wright calls 'consequences' of the action. While the relationship between an action and its result is of a conceptual nature, the relationship between an action and its consequences is of a causal nature. An action necessarily has a result, but it does not necessarily have consequences.

(3) The distinction between results and consequences is relative:

„When I say that I ventilate the room by opening the window, the result of action here is that the window opens (is open). When I say that I open the window by turning the handle, *etc.* , the change in position of the handle, *etc.*, is the result, the change in position of the window the consequence."[31]

This indicates that whether a state of affairs is a result or a consequence of an action depends on the agent's intention:

„When the outer aspect of an action consists of several causally related phases, it is normally correct to single out *one* of them as the *object* of the agent's intention. It is the thing which the agent *intends to do*. This is the result of his action."[32]

[28] Von Wright 1963a, p. 36.

[29] Von Wright 1968, p. 43.

[30] Von Wright 1963a, p. 39.

[31] Von Wright 1971, p. 69.

[32] Ibid., p. 89.

From the thesis of the conceptual relationship between action and result, and the thesis that the result depends on the intention of the agent, it can be inferred that if we want to know what an agent has done we must find out what his intention was. That same thesis is maintained by Jesús Mosterín for whom „every action is intentional. If there is no intention, there is no action, although there may be observable movements. And if we make observable movements with several intentions, then we perform (with these movements) as many different actions as we have different intentions."[33]

In order to illustrate the consequences of that theory, we can use an example that is already well-known in the theory of action, for being highly illustrative: the legend of Oedipus. An oracle predicted to Laius, King of Thebes, and Jocasta, his wife, that they will have a son who will kill his father and marry his mother. When Oedipus was born, he was abandoned by his parents and later adopted by a couple from Corinth. There, another oracle repeated the prophecy to Oedipus and, not knowing that the couple from Corinth were his adoptive parents, he fled the city. On his way, he met Laius who did not want to let him pass, so he killed him, not knowing that he was his real father. When he reached Thebes, he solved the riddle of the Sphinx and as a reward was married to Queen Jocasta, not knowing that she was his mother.

Oedipus's conduct can be described as follows:

(1) Oedipus killed a traveller.
(2) Oedipus killed his father.
(3) Oedipus married Jocasta.
(4) Oedipus married his mother.

For von Wright and Mosterín, only *(1)* and *(3)* describe actions performed by Oedipus, because only they correspond to Oedipus's intentions. Since von Wright does not explain whether non-intentional actions have results and what they are, it seems that we cannot even say that *(2)* and *(4)* were non-intentional actions of Oedipus.[34] And Mosterín explicitly states that *(2)* and *(4)* are consequences of Oedipus's actions, but not themselves actions of his.[35] For these two authors, definitely, only descriptions or interpretations of bodily movements which conform to the intention of the agent are actions. The property that is decisive for the individuation of actions is intention and the change represented in that intention.

Despite its philosophical attractiveness (it fits the traditional view that the teleological or intentional explication of actions is a distinctive feature of the human sciences), the position held by von Wright and Mosterín has a serious disadvantage for ethics and the law: it takes into account only the point of view of the agent himself or of someone who puts himself into the agent's shoes (from the agent's point of view, the most natural interpretation of his bodily movements is the one that takes into account the in-

[33] Mosterín 1983, p. 176.

[34] Although von Wright would certainly say so. The objections to his thesis refer to a problem of indeterminacy concerning non-intentional actions rather than to his treatment of intentional actions.

[35] Mosterín 1983, p. 175.

tention with which he performed it). This theory gives the agent the last word about his actions,[36] but from an *external point of view*, i. e., the point of view of an observer or a 'victim' of the action (or even of the agent in his capacity as an observer or victim of his own action), other descriptions of the respective bodily movements may be relevant. As a consequence of what has been said, it cannot account for what happens with non-intentional actions. In order to do that, we need other criteria of individuation that are independent of the agent's intention.

3. Individuation as Imputation (H. L. A. Hart)

In 1949, H. L. A. Hart published 'The Ascription of Responsibility and Rights' which gave an important impulse to the philosophy of action. In that article, Hart proposed a new approach to statements that refer to actions. Let me quote the relevant passage in his own words:

„There are in our ordinary language sentences whose primary function is not to describe things, events, or persons or anything else, nor to express or kindle feelings or emotions, but to do such things as claim rights ('This is mine'), recognize rights when claimed by others ('Very well, this is yours'), ascribe rights whether claimed or not ('This is his'), transfer rights ('This is now yours'), and also to admit or ascribe or make accusations of responsibility ('I did it', 'He did it', 'You did it'). My main purpose in this article is to suggest that the philosophical analysis of the concept of human action has been inadequate and confused, at least in part because sentences of the form 'He did it' have been traditionally regarded as primarily descriptive, whereas their principal function is what I venture to call ascriptive, being quite literally to ascribe responsibility for actions much as the principal function of sentences of the form 'This is his' is to ascribe right in property."[37]

For Hart, statements ascribing actions are characterized by being 'revocable' or 'defeasible'; he thereby extends to the sphere of action the features which, in his view, belong to legal concepts. He thinks that legal concepts cannot be given precision by specifying a number of conditions that are necessary and jointly sufficient for the validity of the concept. In his opinion, for the definition of a legal concept one needs a (necessarily open) list of exceptions, or negative circumstances, which exclude the application of the concept or stipulate that it be applied in a more moderate or partial form. The concept of contract, for example, is a legal concept that cannot be defined by a number of necessary and sufficient conditions, because even in the case that all the conditions for the validity of a contract hold ('two parties', 'an offer', 'an acceptance', etc.), this can be nullified by a number of negative conditions (error, immoral purposes, etc.). For Hart, the same applies to the concept of action:

„[T]hough of course not all the rules in accordance with which, in our society, we ascribe responsibility are reflected in our legal code nor vice versa, yet our concept of 'action', like our concept of property, is a social concept and logically dependent on accepted rules of conduct. It is fundamentally not descriptive, but ascrip-

[36] Although some caution is warranted, since von Wright seems to suggest at one point that an agent may be mistaken about his own intentions: „My knowledge of my own intentions can be based on reflective knowledge of myself and on observing and putting an interpretation on my reactions. In such cases, knowledge of myself is just as 'external' and 'indirect' as that of another observer, and may be even less reliable than his knowledge of me" (von Wright 1971, p. 114).

[37] Hart 1948/49, p. 145.

tive in character; and it is a defeasible concept to be defined through exceptions and not by a set of necessary and sufficient conditions whether physical or psychological.“[38]

Hart's 'ascriptivist theory' has been the subject of numerous criticisms. Geach and Pitcher, for instance, hold that Hart has fallen victim to an unbalanced 'diet' of examples, paying attention only to those in which a statement of action is equivalent to a reproach, and leaving out examples in which there is no such reproach (as in 'The doctor has just left');[39] years later, Hart himself explicitly rejected the theses of his article.[40] But his suggestion of the ascriptive nature of statements of action can perhaps be rescued, at least for some of them, or for some meaning of 'action'. That is what Joel Feinberg tries to do in his 'Action and responsibility'. The following is a presentation of the essential ideas expressed in that article.

As we have seen, according to Hart statements of the kind 'Alfred did *x*' are not descriptive, but ascriptive or attributive statements, their primary function being the ascription of responsibility to an agent. In order to understand the implications of these assertions, we need some conceptual precision of the meaning of 'ascription' and of 'responsibility'.

The terms 'attribution' or 'ascription' can be understood in a weak or in a strong sense. In the weak sense, 'attributing' or 'ascribing' is equivalent to answering the question 'Who did *x*?'; in that weak sense, the difference between ascriptions and descriptions is the same as that between answering the question 'Who did *x*?' and the question 'What did Alfred do?'. In the strong sense, the ascriptive function of language is different from the descriptive function in that it implies an irreducible degree of discretion (ascription in the strong sense is a matter of *decision* rather than a matter of *discovery*), is relative to the respective context (i. e., our interest in ascribing an action to one agent or other, or to ascribe one action or other to some agent, depends on the context), and it is 'defeasible (i. e., ascriptions are *prima facie*).

Feinberg distinguishes five senses of the expression 'ascription of responsibility':

(1) ascription of a causal relationship: In that sense, 'Alfred was responsible for *x*' is equivalent to saying that *x* was the causal result of Alfred's action, without implying any judgment of the action;

(2) ascription of causal agency: Feinberg notes that, because of the 'accordion effect', ascriptions of responsibility in the merely causal sense to an agent can be replaced by ascriptions of agency (as we have seen, 'Alfred caused the door to close' and 'Alfred closed the door' may be equivalent);

(3) ascriptions of simple agency: This is the ascription of agency of a simple or basic action (in the sense of Arthur Danto, mentioned above), i. e., an action that cannot be performed by way of another action – like lifting an arm, smiling, etc. – is ascribed to an agent. Feinberg sees the relationship between an agent and his simple actions as a

[38] Ibid. p. 161.

[39] Cf. Nino 1987, p. 18.

[40] Cf. the Preface in Hart 1973.

peculiar, non-causal relationship; hence, ascriptions of simple agency cannot be translated into ascriptions of merely causal responsibility;

(4) imputations of fault: This is the ascription to an agent of an action that is, to some extent and in some sense (technically, legally, morally, etc.), judged to be blameworthy;

(5) ascription of strict liability: This is the ascription of liability understood as 'sanctionability' or 'liability to be sanctioned', i. e., a person is attributed the condition of being a sufferer of the (normative) consequences deriving from the fact that a certain action has been performed (by that person or another agent).[41]

Once these five cases have been distinguished, we recognize that there is always *some* sense of 'responsibility' (but not always the same) and *some* sense of 'ascription' (but not always the same) for which it is true that statements of action ascribe responsibility, and there are four cases in which ascriptions in the strong sense are made. There is no doubt about those cases where a blameworthy action, or responsibility in the strict sense, is ascribed to someone (in these cases, there is an evaluation of the action and a *decision* about whether or not a sanction should be imposed). But all the other cases may raise doubts. Feinberg holds that there is also an ascription in the strong sense when we ascribe only causal responsibility or causal agency to an agent, because to determine the cause of some outcome is not merely a descriptive question: from a number of different events, all of which are necessary or contributing conditions of the effect (i. e. they are what could be called its 'causal context'), one must be chosen as *the* cause (usually, it is the element that is 'anormal in the context').[42] This choice is a matter of decision (that is, it has an irreducible degree of discretion), it is contextual, and it is revocable. The only case where there is no ascription in the strong sense is that of the ascription of simple agency: „Whether or not a man smiled is enterely a question of fact whose answer is to be discovered, not 'decided' or 'selected' presumptively.“[43]

As we have seen, the theory of Hart and Feinberg suggests that the concept of action is a social concept, i. e., that the criteria for determining (ascribing) what action someone has performed (or, in Goldman's terms, what properties we focus on to individuate an action) depend on social, moral, legal, etc., conventions and rules. For these authors, all cases of the individuation of an action, except those of the individuation of a simple action, are instances of ascription in the strong sense. But, again, there is a problem with this theory: An ascriptivist (in the strong sense) theory of action is a theory that interprets actions from the point of view of others, not from the point of view of the agent himself. It makes sense to say that the observer of a bodily movement attributes or ascribes or imputes an action to an agent in the strong sense, i. e., in a discretional, contextual and defeasible way; but it makes no sense to say that the agent attributes or

41 Hart too later referred to that sense of responsibility (as well as to responsibility as a causal relation): „To say that someone is legally responsible for something often means only that under legal rules he is liable to be made either to suffer or to pay compensation in certain eventualities“ (Hart 1973, p. 196). On the concept of responsibility in Hart (and in other authors) in general, cf., e. g., Larrañaga Monjaraz (forthcoming).

42 Cf. below, Chapter VII, sect. 4.1.

43 Feinberg 1968, p. 116.

ascribes or imputes an action to himself in a discretional, contextual, and defeasible way. If he does, it would be more adequate to say that he has taken the position of an observer.

Hence, the ascriptivist theory takes another standpoint than von Wright's theory. And by doing so, just as von Wright in his theory cannot adequately account for non-intentional actions, Hart cannot adequately account for intentional actions, unless we would be willing to accept that we ascribe (in the strong sense) intentions to agents (and even that agents ascribe intentions to themselves). But that would be a mistake, as I will try to show with an example:

Suppose I am walking along the street and I see a friend approaching who lifts his arm. I am not sure whether he has seen me and is lifting his arm to greet me or whether he is simply flagging down a taxi. If I want to determine what he is doing, I must put myself in his place and find out what his intention is. There are many cases in which we try to find out the intentions of others in order to determine what they have been doing. And in order to find out the intention of a person, it is helpful to know about certain rules and regularities of conduct (like the one saying that lifting an arm can be a way of greeting); but even then, what we are doing in such cases is more like a descriptive than an ascriptive use of language, more a matter of 'discovering' or 'reconstructing' the intention of the agent than of 'deciding' what it was. This becomes clear if we remember that when we try to individuate an action according to the agent's intention, we are willing to admit that we were wrong if later the agent tells us (convincingly) that his intention had been another. In such cases, we do allow the agent to have the last word about his action. In contrast, this is not the case when we ascribe an action in the strong sense. In those cases, the agent's own sincere word is not enough: in order to be cleared of responsibility, the subject to whom we ascribe an action must either deny that there is any sense at all in which he has acted or, if he can, employ his arsenal of excuses and justifications.[44]

4. Some Conclusions

From the preceding analysis, we can now draw some preliminary conclusions:

(1) The controversy between Davidson and Goldman about the individuation of actions is not restricted to the question of counting actions. Rather, it is based on two different ways of constructing the concept of action. Perhaps we can generalize this and say that a solution to the problems of individuation presupposes choosing certain conceptual options. We cannot individuate an entity if we do not have a concept that allows

[44] However, there are some exceptions to the assertion that we do not attribute intentions or intentional actions to agents. In the law, occasionally there are presumptions that can be interpreted as the attribution of an intention to an agent, regardless of his real intention. But such strong attributions of intention are usually connected with problems in proving what the agent's real intention was. This connection with questions of proof (that is, of fact) again shows that our approach to the intentions of others is more like an attempt to discover what there intentions are than like an imputation of intentions according to some social rules, regardless of their intention in a psychological sense.

us to identify the respective kind of entities. In that sense, we can even go one step further and say that the theories of Davidson and Goldman are not primarily theories about the individuation of actions (note that neither does Davidson indicate how the sequence of bodily movements that constitutes an action is to be delimited, nor does Goldman tell us how to determine the number of act-properties a person exemplifies at a given time), but focused on an earlier stage, to wit, on the concept of action.

(2) The alternative represented by Davidson and Goldman for the construction of a notion of action is the following: either action is understood as an observable fact or as a theoretical construct (like magnetic fields or entropy, as Jesús Mosterín[45] notes). From the former point of view, action is identified with a sequence of bodily movements that can be described or interpreted in some way or other; from the latter point of view, it is identified with bodily movements plus a certain interpretation or meaning depending on one or several of the properties they exemplify.

(3) In turn, once one opts for considering actions as the sum of a voluntary bodily movement and one of its possible interpretations (action-interpretation), the theories of von Wright and Hart can be seen as proposals of different criteria for the interpretation of bodily movements: the intention of the agent, and social rules, respectively.

(4) If we take the theories of Davidson, von Wright and Hart as points of reference, it may be useful to treat them not as three rival theories about the concept of action, but as complementary theories pointing to three different aspects of actions. Whenever we act, we can distinguish *(i)* the movements of our body (Davidson), *(ii)* that which we are intentionally doing in performing those bodily movements (von Wright), and *(iii)* the relevant social consequences of *(ii)* (Hart). Using Arthur Danto's notion of a basic action and von Wright's distinction between results and consequences, we can call these three aspects of actions the 'basic act', the 'result-act', and the'consequence-act'.[46]

[45] Mosterín 1993, p. 176.

[46] I will have more to say about this distinction in Chapter VI.

CHAPTER IV

THE DEBATE IN CRIMINAL LAW

1. Introduction

In the previous chapter, I have tried to show that the debate about the individuation of actions (one of the most relevant, but not the only debate about action in the sphere of the philosophy of action) revolves around three different aspects of actions, and that rather than focusing exclusively on one of these aspects, it may be more fruitful to construct a theory of action with three levels, which take into account each one of those aspects, respectively. In this chapter, I attempt to show that a lack of distinction between the three aspects (or, more precisely, the reduction of the phenomenon of action to only one of them) also underlies some controversies that have taken place within Continental criminal law (and to some extent also in Anglo-Saxon law, to which I will refer more briefly). In Continental criminal law, besides the problems that are intrinsic to the concept of action, we encounter some additional difficulties:

First of all, on many occasions the discussion among criminal lawyers has been plagued by the attempt to derive a number of normative consequences from an assumed ontological structure of action. As we have seen in Chapter I, the concept of action can be useful for the criminal law insofar as it enables one to treat many of the problems in that branch of the law in a generic fashion. If legislation on criminal matters must give answers to questions such as the localization of a crime in space and time, the determination of whether someone has committed one or several offences at the same time, or the determination of the mode in which an offence was committed (voluntarily or involuntarily, by omission, ...), etc., the availability of a common concept of action makes it possible to give one general answer instead of particular answers for each and every prohibited kind of action. But some of the traditional theories of action elaborated by lawyers have gone a step further and claimed not only that the concept of action serves to give a generic answer to such questions, but also that it serves to determine what the answer should be. That is, they have tried to ground normative conclusions on a description of the 'nature of action'. In most cases, however, that is asking too much of the concept of action which, on the contrary, must be constructed, or reconstructed, precisely in the light of the normative criteria with which the problems are to be solved.[1]

Another problem is raised by the fact that the definition of an offence, in criminal dogmatics, as a typified, unlawful and culpable action transfers to the legal sphere some elements that can be regarded as belonging to a prelegal, common concept

[1] On the problems a conceptualist approach (holding that normative solutions can be derived from the combination of the different elements of an offence) or a realist approach (holding that there is such a thing as a real, objective definition of action and of crime) raises in the criminal-law doctrine, cf., e. g., Nino 1980, pp. 64 ff.

of action. The requirement that a crime must be typified is equivalent to the requirement that an individual act – or, in the terminology of Alvin Goldman, an act-token – must exemplify a property, i. e., that it must belong to a category of actions or an act-type; and the requirement of culpability, in its two forms of intent or negligence, is linked to the requirement that an action must be accompanied by a volition (which some philosophers deem necessary to distinguish actions from mere bodily movements, such as reflex acts). If these elements are necessary for an adequate definition of 'action', we must be cautious with statements of the kind „The concept of action must not contain elements that belong to the other characteristics of a crime", because if that were the case „it would give rise to a twisted system in which the substantive (action) would already partially contain the predicates (typicity, unlawfulness, culpability, sanctionability), and these would therefore end up referring to themselves".[2] If we want to understand this statement correctly, we must remember that types of offences are not the only types of actions, and that culpability is only one particular species of the genus of voluntariness. Hence, from the definition of action we must exclude all references to types of offences, but not to types of actions in general, and, likewise, all reference to culpability, but not to other forms of voluntariness.

Finally, a third source of difficulties, related to the second, is the fact that it is not always clear whether the definitions proposed by some criminal lawyers are meant to refer to a prelegal and precriminal concept of action or to a concept of action that applies only to the criminal law (such as the concept proposed by Maihofer who holds that „action is a human behaviour aimed at causing harm to goods protected by the criminal law"[3]).

2. The Definition of 'Action' in Criminal-Law Doctrine

2.1. The causal theory of action. The trilemma of causalism

In a recently published book, Tomás Vives Antón has given another 'turn of the screw' to what can be called 'the criminal lawyers' theory of action'. In what follows, I will summarize his presentation and critique of theories of action, and analyze his own proposal.[4]

Following majority opinion, Vives Antón locates the origin of the analysis of the concept of action in the criminal law in Hegel's philosophy of law. Hegel proposes a concept of action that is intrinsically linked to a valuation from a normative point of view. Action is for Hegel „the exteriorization of the will as subjective or moral".[5] On

2 Rodríguez Mourullo 1966, p. 221, quoted from Cobo del Rosal/Vives Antón 1984, p. 320.

3 Quoted from Gimbernat Ordeig 1990, p. 121.

4 In presenting the causal, teleological and social theories of action, I will refer to their most radical versions, in order to bring out more clearly the differences between them and to underscore the thesis of the present investigation. I am aware of the fact that there are less radical versions of each one of these theories to which some of the criticisms I will mention do not apply.

5 Quoted from Vives Antón 1996, p. 103.

this point, Hegel and his followers have indeed been interpreted as defending what we could call a concept of 'criminal action', not applicable to the prelegal sphere, according to which only conducts which violate a duty are actions. But such a concept leads to serious problems, even if it is understood as a definition meant to apply only in the sphere of the criminal law. By regarding as legally relevant only conducts that imply the violation of a duty, everything done by persons who are not subject to legal duties (such as children or the mentally deranged) is excluded from the concept of action.[6]

One has therefore tried to find a prelegal concept of action which alone, it is said, can fulfil the functions expected from this concept in the criminal law. According to Vives Antón, these functions are: a negative function („If crime is, first of all, action, then an immediate consequence is that what is not action can therefore not be a crime"[7]), a classificatory function („Action must be the common genus from which the different species of offences: active and omissive, intentional and negligent, can be distinguished"[8]), a coordinating function („If action is the substantive from which the other characters of an offence – of being unlawful, culpable and sanctionable – are predicated as adjectives, it must obviously constitute a *link* between them and *cannot anticipate its content* without giving rise to a flagrant tautology"[9]), and a defining function („If action is the substance which, in order to be an offence, must be characterized by attributes consisting basically in unlawfulness and culpability, then it must provide the material substrate of both of them, that is, it must contain elements on which a judgment of disvalue and a judgment of blame can be pronounced"[10]). An important consequence that can be drawn from these functions is that if one is looking for a concept of action that may be of use for the criminal law, this must not be so narrow as to include any one of the other defining elements of an offence, nor so broad as to include conducts on which it is impossible to express a value-judgment (which, in the terminology introduced in the previous chapter, is equivalent to saying that it must be a concept of interpreted and not of basic action).[11]

An attempt to overcome the problems of Hegel's theory of action can be found in the so-called causal theory of action. Tomás Vives links this theory to the positivist attitude which at some point has been spreading in the social sciences, in their urgent desire to hold their own as scientific enterprises on a par with the natural sciences. Translated to the criminal law, that attitude implies „to characterize a crime, above all, as *something that exists* in the world ('social facts must be considered things',

[6] Ibid.

[7] Ibid. p. 106.

[8] Ibid. p. 105.

[9] Ibid. p. 105.

[10] Ibid. p. 106.

[11] An example of an action on which no value-judgment can be passed is the following: „If one starts from a conception which describes the 'substance' of the offence of falsification of documents as consisting in producing or erasing ink-spots on a piece of paper, then with that description one has not provided any ground on which judgments of unlawfulness and culpability can be based, since one has not identified anything that could as such be the object of an assessment of disvalue or of blame" (ibid. p. 106).

according to Durkheim's famous phrase), that is, as an *action*, or, still further, as a *fact*, to insist on its nature of *reality*, on its *psycho-physical* aspects, that is, emphasizing the purely *ontical* over the *normative*".[12] Holding on to this purpose, the causal theory defines action as „the voluntary production or non-avoidance of an external change in the world".[13] Von Liszt, one of its main representatives, thinks that action is „any material modification, even an insignificant one, of the external world that is perceptible through the senses".[14]

For the causal theory, action therefore consists of an internal and an external phase. The internal phase is constituted by a desire or volition; the external phase is constituted by a change in the world. Thus, there is an action whenever a change in the world has been brought about by a will (regardless of its content). That change can be merely a bodily movement or something more complex. In other words, voluntary bodily movements are actions just as much as the voluntary production of a change other than those bodily movements. Although the definition of action refers to voluntariness, what is relevant for the causal theory is its presence, not its *content* (which, in contrast, is relevant for the determination of culpability).

According to Tomás Vives, this kind of definitions of 'action' have several inconveniences. The first is that, although the causal theory of action claims to account for omissions as well as actions proper, it can in fact only do so by introducing two definitions (referring to 'production' and to 'non-avoidance'), which means that there is no single concept of action (in the broad sense). The second objection against the causal theory of action is that in this theory mere voluntary movements of the body are already regarded as actions, although action descriptions in terms of bodily movements do not carry enough information to make them the subject of evaluation and possibly of blame. No criminal code prohibits actions which consist only in some bodily movements, such as moving the fingers of a hand, lifting an arm, making noises with one's mouth, or drawing little ink-spots on a piece of paper. In order to evaluate a conduct or to determine whether it falls under some provision of the law, those bodily movements must be described in the light of some of the circumstances in which they were made and of the consequences they brought about. In the words of Tomás Vives: „If action is defined in such a way that it sometimes describes purely neutral processes which can be considered neither evil nor blameworthy, such a definition must be discarded."[15]

This objection is, in fact, even more serious than Tomás Vives recognizes: for him, the problem is that some of the things the causal theory calls 'actions' (i. e., bodily movements) cannot be evaluated. But the main problem of the causal theory is that it faces a trilemma: either it says that all changes originating in an agent's will are actions (which seems exaggerated since the causal chains might be infinite); or it provides criteria by which the causal chains generated (through bodily movements) by an agent's will can be cut off (which means that the purpose of offering a purely naturalistic theory

[12] Ibid. p. 104.

[13] Ibid. p. 107.

[14] Quoted from Welzel 1947, p. 34.

[15] Vives Antón 1996, p. 106.

of action must be abandoned and the theory becomes teleological or social); or it holds that only voluntary movements of the body are actions (which makes it fall squarely under Vives's criticism).

In fact, we have seen that for the causal theory an action is the voluntary production (or non-avoidance) of a change. Now, when the will triggers a causal process that leads to the production of a change, it is at the root of a chain of consequences that may be infinite. According to the causal theory, the sequential structure of action can be represented as follows (where I = intention, BM = bodily movement, C = consequence):

$$I — BM — C_1 —— C_2 —— C_3 —— ... —— C_n$$

With this illustration, we immediately see that in order to determine whether, e. g., C_3 is to be considered a change in the world produced by the will or intention of some agent (that is, a change in the world which gives rise to an action), the causal theory must be complemented with a theory of causality (or, if you like, a theory of causality *in action*, that is, a theory answering to the question what consequences must be regarded as the effects of a particular will). If that theory states that any consequence which, in the last instance, originates in the respective will can give rise to an action, we are dealing with the first horn of the trilemma (that is what happens if one adopts the theory known by criminal lawyers as the theory of the equivalence of conditions, because that theory cannot cut off the causal chain; according to it, „all facts prior to the production of the typified result, however remote their relation to it may be, are causes“[16]). If that theory does introduce limits to the causal chain, then, because these limits refer either to the agent's intention (as, we will see, is the case of the teleological theory) or to social criteria (as in the case of the social theory), the causal theory cannot be a naturalistic theory, and we are facing the second horn of the trilemma (that is what happens with the adequacy theory and the relevance theory, which attempt to cut off the chain with the help of criteria that are not naturalistic, such as that of the adequacy of the cause to bring about the result, or that of the relevance of the cause according to some disposition of the criminal code[17] The only alternative left to the causal theory of action is to say that only bodily movements are actions, which takes us to the third horn of the trilemma.

2.2. THE TELEOLOGICAL THEORY OF ACTION. THE PARTIAL ABANDONING OF TELEOLOGY

An attempt to overcome the problems of Hegel's theory while avoiding the defects of the causal theory is the so-called teleological theory of action proposed by Hans Welzel. Welzel holds that „all moral and legal norms can only refer to acts, which are different from mere causal processes in that they are distinguished from them by the element of a conscious direction towards a goal, that is, by the element of *teleology*. The (teleological) structure of human action is the precondition for the possibility to evaluate an action“.[18] Therefore, for Welzel „human action is the exercise of a purposive activity.

[16] Cobo del Rosal/Vives Antón 1984, p. 348.

[17] On these criteria, cf., e. g., Gómez Benítez 1988, pp. 22 ff.

[18] Welzel 1951, p. 244.

Hence, action is a 'teleological', and not only a 'causal' phenomenon [...] purpose is based on the capacity of the will to foresee to some extent the consequences of a causal intervention, and thus direct it purposefully towards the goal".[19]

Seen from the standpoint of the criminal law, the teleological theory, as I said, claims to solve the problems of the causal theory by providing a concept of action that permits us to evaluate actions and to contrast them from types of offences. But the teleological theory can also be seen from a point of view that is external to the criminal law. From that perspective, the difference between the causal and the teleological theory can be understood to fall within the framework of the difference between two traditions about the nature of scientific explanation: the Galilean tradition (leading to the positivism that inspires the causal theory), for which there is one single model of scientific explanation, common to all the different types of sciences, according to which the phenomenon to be explained is subsumed under a general causal law (social phenomena can thus be reduced to natural phenomena); and the Aristotelian tradition (leading to the attempt to set off the social sciences against the natural sciences which seems to inspire the teleological theory of action), for which the social sciences are characterized by the study of phenomena which have a sense or meaning that must be explained from an intentional or teleological point of view.[20]

For Welzel, the agent's intention or the content of his will not only encompasses the goal sought by the agent, but also the means employed in its pursuit, and the „secondary consequences that are necessarily linked to the use of the means".[21] However, despite this expansion, the teleological theory of action cannot account for negligent actions or offences, because actions performed negligently are, by definition, actions not directed towards the result that has been brought about, i. e., they are not actions directed towards some purpose. To account for those actions, Welzel refers to a „potential purpose" of negligent acts,[22] or he says that concerning these offences, the purpose pursued is irrelevant for the criminal law.

Now, by saying that in the case of offences of negligence the content of the intention is irrelevant for the criminal law, the definition of action is reformulated *ad hoc*, in a way that makes the definition of action for offences of negligence coincide with the definition of the causal theory (there is an action whenever a change in the world is produced by a volition, regardless of its content). Hence, here the trilemma appears again with respect to offences of negligence.

2.3. THE SOCIAL THEORY OF ACTION. ITS INSUFFICIENCY

Remember that the trilemma consists in that either the causal theory identifies actions with bodily movements; or it must struggle with a concept of action that goes toward infinity; or it abandons its aspiration of being a naturalistic theory and adopts a

[19] Welzel 1947, p. 28.

[20] On these two traditions, cf. von Wright 1971, ch. 1; also Mardones 1991.

[21] Welzel 1947, p. 29.

[22] Vives Antón 1996, p. 109.

normative theory of causality which allows it to cut off the chain of consequences (or adopts intentionalism). The social theory of action opts for that last alternative. In fact, some authors have pointed out that the social theory confounds a theory of action with a theory of causality or of the causal imputation of results. Thus, Welzel holds (referring specifically to the social theory of Maihofer) that it „only offers a new name for something that is already old (the adequacy theory) and whose problems end precisely where those of the doctrine of action begin“.[23] But that identification – rather than confusion – is inevitable since, because of the 'accordion effect' of actions, we can say either 'Alfred caused Peter's death' or 'Alfred killed Peter'. Only when we have put a limit to the 'accordion' of the causal chain generated by an agent's will (i. e., when we have established 'how far the action goes') does it make sense to ask where the theory of action ends and a theory of the causal imputation of consequences begins.

In order to cut off the causal chain, the social theory takes recourse to social criteria. The backbone of the social theory of action is spelled out very well in the following statement by Maihofer: „The starting point for the classification of a behaviour as an action is the social community.“[24] The social theory of action, Vives Antón and Cobo del Rosal write, „does not content itself with the purely naturalistic account of the causal theory, nor does it adopt the subjectivism of the intentionalist postulates. It emphasizes, correctly, the social nature of human action. Human action can be understood only by taking into account the social context in which it emerges“.[25] As Tomás Vives has noted, the social theory brings up the idea of the social 'sense' or meaning of an action; thus, in the words of E. Schmidt, who was the first to formulate it, „unless one adopts a hyperindividualistic (or even a solipsistic) point of view, one must recognize that from the social environment in which they are developed (from the life sphere of the 'others') and because of that social contact, the different ways of conduct receive a *sense* which neither the *thinking* nor the *will* of the author by themselves can determine“.[26]

From this perspective, action has been defined as „every conduct that can objectively be dominated and that is directed towards an objectively foreseeable social result“ (Maihofer) or „all socially relevant human behaviour“ (Jescheck).[27]

One of the criticisms that have been expressed against this concept of action is that it ends up defining action in terms of what is prohibited in the law, and fails to provide a prelegal concept of action. The reason for this is that the clearest criterion for the determination of which consequences of the causal chain are relevant for the criminal law is to find out whether any of the consequences are described in the law. In other words: the law itself is the clearest criterion of the social relevance (of the kind of social relevance that matters for the criminal law) of an action.

[23] Quoted from Jaén Vallejo 1994, p. 58.

[24] Quoted from Vives Antón 1996, p. 114.

[25] Cobo del Rosal/Vives Antón 1984, p. 319.

[26] Quoted from Vives Antón 1996, p. 115.

[27] The quotes are taken from Jaén Vallejo 1994, pp. 57 and 58.

Another problem raised by the social theory is that it cannot account for all actions that are relevant for the criminal law, because it requires that an action has a sense, similar to that of the teleological theory: many actions acquire their meaning precisely on the basis of the content of the will. That is Jescheck's opinion when he says that a purely objective conception of the social is too narrow, „since the concept of action must encompass forms of conduct which receive their purposiveness from the author's will“[28] and not from more or less objective social criteria. This statement shows that the social theory is insufficient for explaining intentional actions where it is precisely the presence and the content of the intention which gives sense to an action. We will come back to this problem in examining the next theory.

2.4. A NEW VERSION OF THE SOCIAL THEORY: THE THEORY OF ACTION AS MEANING

Tomás Vives himself has proposed a theory of action which, he believes, is not plagued by the problems encountered in the theories we have seen so far. He calls it the „conception of action as meaning“. As we have seen, some authors who advocate the social theory have suggested a parallel, albeit a metaphorical one, between the theory of action and the theory of language, in speaking of the 'sense' of an action. Starting from the thesis that actions have a sense or meaning, Tomás Vives, instead of searching for the substrate or the subject of that meaning (as the social theory claims to be doing), proposes that action is *precisely that meaning*: „This brings about a Copernican turn in the theory of action: it is no longer the *substrate of a sense*, but, inversely, the *sense of a substrate*“.[29] Thus, actions are „the social meaning of a conduct“, the „interpretations that, according to different kinds of social rules, can be given of human behaviour“;[30] and what distinguishes facts from actions is that „facts happen, actions make sense (that is, they *mean something*); facts can be described, actions must be understood; facts are explained by physical, chemical, biological, etc., laws, actions are interpreted with the help of rules of grammar“.[31]

I think, however, that this conception of 'action as meaning' has some problems:

(1) The first problem is that from this perspective actions do not exist (just as for Hart's ascriptivist conception of action of which the conception of Thomás Vives can be seen as a new version[32]). At least, they do not exist in a strong sense, as natural phenomena. This consequence is acknowledged by Vives, who says that „meaning does not *exist*, it is not a class of objects of the world which we perceive, it only means something“.[33] Thus, the conception of action as meaning 'solves' the first of the paradoxes we have seen in Chapter II by denying that actions are natural phenomena. It is therefore one of those skeptical theories Michael S. Moore referred to. But to deny

[28] Quoted from ibid. p. 58.

[29] Vives Antón 1996, p. 205.

[30] Ibid.

[31] Ibid.

[32] Cf. above, Chapter III, sect. 3.

[33] Vives Antón 1996, p. 208.

that actions exist as physical phenomena is a counterintuitive consequence which we should accept only if there is no alternative.

An analogy with the concept of norm can give us a glimpse of what that alternative, which permits us to link actions with the physical world and still uphold that they have meaning, could be: syntactically, norms are sometimes identified with norm-sentences ('norm-formulations'); semantically, they are identified with the meaning of norm-sentences; and from a mixed point of view, some authors have proposed a notion according to which norms are not simply sentences, nor simply meanings, but meaningful sentences, i. e., sentences provided with a certain, constant meaning.[34] Similarly, one can say that an action is not a mere sequence of bodily movements, nor the meaning of such bodily movements. Rather, it is movements of the body *with* a certain meaning.

Related to this problem is the fact that the definition of action as 'the social meaning of a conduct' includes a partial synonym of action ('conduct') which remains undefined. The conception of action as meaning, thus, cannot do without referring to another sense of action (which coincides with what in Chapter VI I will call 'basic act').

(2) The second difficulty is that Vives Antón overstretches the analogy between the meaning of linguistic utterances and the meaning of our actions (although, certainly, it is a very illuminating analogy), without saying what he understands by either one of these meanings. The parallel between the theory of action and the theory of meaning has its limits. On the one hand, the category of what we call 'meaning' in language includes very different things, and one would need to specify for which of these the analogy holds. As we will see in Chapter V, one thing is the meaning of what can be called a 'sentence-type' or 'utterance-type' (which is 'timeless' and depends on certain rules of grammar and conventions) and quite another the meaning of 'utterance-tokens', that is, of our linguistic utterances made at a certain time and in a certain context (which is an 'occasion-meaning' that is not only a function of the meaning of the words contained in the utterance, but depends also on that other kind of meaning stipulated by the rules of grammar, on certain rather vague conventions referring to the context in which the utterance is made, as well as on the *intentions of the speaker*).[35] On the other hand, the meaning of our linguistic utterances is something we attempt to communicate (or, according to John Searle, to represent), whereas the meaning of our actions does not always have that link to communication: to speak is to attempt to communicate or represent something, but to act is to attempt to change the world (and only for the class of actions we call 'speaking' or 'saying something' it is also an attempt to communicate or represent something). As I will argue later, what we call the 'sense' or 'meaning' of an action is what permits us to classify certain bodily movements as one or another kind of action, not what we communicate through them (if we communicate anything at all).

[34] Cf. Bulygin 1986, Sect. 2; Alchourrón 1986, p. 173.

[35] On this important distinction, cf., e. g., Grice 1989a, pp. 88 ff.; see also Grice 1971. Below, I give an example that may help to understand the distinction.

(3) The third problem with this conception, related to the distinction between 'timeless meaning' and 'occasion-meaning' can be seen in the following passage by Tomás Vives:

„We can speak of actions only if subjects have the capacity to form and express intentions; however, the actions they perform do not depend on the interntions they are supposed to express, but on the meaning socially attributed to what they do. The analogy with language may be illuminating here: there is language only if subjects want to say something; but the meaning of what they say does not depend on what they want to say with it, but on the sense that, in accordance with the 'grammar' of the language they express themselves in, must be attributed to their expressions."[36]

Vives illustrates these statements with the following examples taken from Wittgenstein: „Thus, one can naturally imagine that in a tribe that does not know the game two people sit down in front of a chessboard and go through the motions of playing a game [...] and if *we* saw it, we would think that they are playing chess".[37] According to this passage – which contains an idea the author repeats on many occasions, although on others he qualifies it –, the meaning of an action is independent of the intention (understood as the subjective mental state) of the agent who performs it and is determined exclusively – or, at least, basically – by social rules. Of course, this does not imply that Vives Antón ignores intentional action; it implies that for him what matters is not intention understood as a subjective state, but as a sense which we *attribute* to an action: „Hence, there is an external, *objective* 'intentionality', a social practice which constitutes the meaning – that which the advocates of the social theory of action called 'objective finality'".[38]

A theory based on social rules and 'objective' or 'external' intention has the problem that it is a partial, incomplete theory, because it forgets the relevance of 'subjective' intentions,[39] ignoring the 'agent's point of view'. I will try to show the importance of that standpoint (for the theory of linguistic meaning as well as for the theory of the meaning of an action) with the following example:

Suppose I have gone to a party with my wife. I must confess that I don't like to dance (I have good reason to suspect that I would make a fool of myself if I tried); my wife, in contrast, loves to dance (and she's an excellent dancer); therefore, she usually leaves me standing at the bar with a drink while she looks for someone to dance with. I'm a very understanding person so we have never quarrelled about this – she likes to dance, and I like to have a drink. Tonight, however, things are not going as they should. My wife has been dancing for too long with always the same individual, who is too tall, too elegant and too attractive for me to keep calm, but who looks vaguely familiar to me. While I observe them, I realize that the man's hand moves down my wife's back to

[36] Vives Antón 1996, p. 214.

[37] Ibid. p. 218.

[38] Ibid. p. 219.

[39] As can be seen in the chess example, Tomás Vives makes no reference whatsoever to the standpoint of the agents (thus adopting a position that is totally opposed to that of the teleological theory, though equally radical) who obviously could not say that they are playing chess. However, the agent's point of view is too important to be left aside by a theory of action.

places where I do not think it reasonable for it to move. Besides, in that same instant I remember that this man is, of all people, a top manager in the company I work for, unbearably arrogant but influential, with whom I would rather stay on good terms. In view of the inexorable progress of the guy's hands, I get nervous, down my drink in one big gulp, resolutely approach the dancing couple and, taking advantage of a pause in the music, say to him: 'Sir, may I introduce my wife to you'.

What does 'May I introduce my wife to you' mean here? Usually, this expression is used as a formula of courtesy, to introduce one person to another; that is the 'normal' or 'literal' or 'timeless' meaning of the sentence; but my utterance of these same words can also be interpreted as an indirect speech act[40] by which I actually want to say 'You better leave my wife alone'. So what does it mean in the example (what is the occasion-meaning of the sentence)? There are good reasons to think that it means both: on the one hand, I got jealous and one might think that I have decided to bring that dance to an end; on the other, I am interested in remaining on good terms with the man and one might also think that I decided to be friendly with him. In that example, thus, *social rules and conventions do not allow an observer to know with certainty what the meaning of my utterance was* and, therefore, what action I have performed (note that in our example there are not only two possible meanings of one and the same utterance, but also two possible actions: depending on which meaning we attribute to the utterance, it is an act of courtesy or an expression of disapproval).

I am tempted to say that what those words *really* or *truly* mean depends on my intention in uttering them: that linguistic conventions only have the function to help those who hear it to interpret the sentence and to allow me to express my intention. But I prefer not to give in to that temptation, because I doubt that it makes sense to speak of the real or true meaning of an utterance. Even so, the example shows that there are several senses of 'meaning' (here, again, one could repeat the distinction between the speaker's point of view and the others' point of view in order to classify those senses), and at least one of them depends (not exclusively, but partly) on what the speaker wants to say, i. e., on his real intentions. That is the sense that is lost in the theory of Vives. But without it, human communication would be very difficult, because *it is not the task of linguistic conventions to objectivize the meaning of our words even at the expense of our intentions, but to allow us to express what we intend to express*.

The question we can now pose is whether perhaps a theory of action that adopts an 'objective' sense of intention, like the one proposed by Tomás Vives, is useful for the law, although it is incomplete for a general theory of human action. It could be argued, for instance, that judges must sometimes establish whether or not a defendant acted intentionally, and in that case they cannot simply 'rely on' his word, but must use their knowledge of society and the world we live in in order to determine whether there was in fact such an intention. Hence, it might be concluded that in such a case the judge attributes an intention to the defendant in accordance with certain criteria. However, I think that we must be very cautious with the conclusion to be drawn from this kind of argument. In my view, the workings of the law are reflected more exactly if we say that rules and conventions help us to 'discover' the intention of the defendant, rather than to

[40] Cf. Searle 1979b.

'attribute' an intention to him, in the strong sense. That this is true is shown by the fact that a judge would commit a serious pragmatic contradiction if she were to convict a defendant for having intentionally (in the objective sense) done *x* although she is convinced that he did not have the intention (in the subjective sense) of doing *x* (take an example from science fiction: suppose a method has been found, a kind of reader for brain waves, to measure the real, subjective intentions of agents). In other words, Tomás Vives seems to identify intention with what are actually only criteria for discovering intention.

3. The Treatment of Action in Anglo-Saxon Law

There are two aspects in the works on the concept of action to be found in Anglo-Saxon law which contrast from those we find in Continental law: On the one hand, they are less abstract and formalistic – Nino even speaks of an 'intuitionist approach'[41] –, which is indicated by a greater number of investigations about specific topics (such as the role of intention in some particular offence) and a smaller number of studies on the concept of action as such.[42] On the other, the separation apparent in Continental law between a 'philosophers' theory of action' and a 'lawyers' theory of action' does not exist, or is at least less pronounced. Thus, it is not uncommon for lawyers to venture into traditionally philosophical territory, or for philosophers to discuss problems traditionally (in the Continental tradition) considered to be legal questions.
Despite these different standpoints, there are also some parallels concerning the topics discussed, in the context of the concept of action, in the two traditions. For example, a certain parallel can be seen between the difference some Anglo-Saxon lawyers have noted between the *act requirement* and what they call the *actus reus requirement* (although these names do not refer to two theories about action) and the discussion about whether a notion of action in naturalistic terms as the one proposed by the causal theory is adequate for the purposes of the law; and the discussion among Anglo-Saxon authors about whether an objectivist or a subjectivist approach to liability is more adequate also has a certain parallel in the controversy between the teleological and the social theory of action.

3.1. *ACT REQUIREMENT* AND *ACTUS REUS REQUIREMENT*. THE ORTHODOX THEORY OF ACTION

The distinction that is of central importance for the delimitation of criminal liability in the Anglo-Saxon tradition is the one drawn between *actus reus* and *mens rea*. The *actus reus* encompasses all the objective and external circumstances of fact required for

[41] For a detailed presentation of the differences between the treatment of criminal liability in Continental law and in Anglo-Saxon law, cf., e. g., Nino 1980, chs. I and II.

[42] Nino 1980, pp. 189 ff., points out the problems caused by the lack of systematic studies of the concept of action (and, in general, on criminal liability) and its more casuistic treatment in Anglo-Saxon law (which he calls 'the informal fallacy').

criminal liability, whereas the *mens rea* covers the subjective and mental circumstances (note that the distinction is in many aspects analogous to the one drawn by continental lawyers between typicity and culpability, although there are also some differences which I will not go into here[43]).

The *actus reus* can actually be seen as a label encompassing two different kinds of conditions: the first condition stipulates that there is no offence if there has been no voluntary act (what is usually called the 'voluntary act requirement'); the second condition stipulates that the act must be an *actus reus*, that is, an act having the properties required in the description of some action as given in a valid norm of the criminal law (the '*actus reus* requirement').[44]

As Hart has noted, in Anglo-Saxon criminal law there is a General Doctrine concerning the two conditions (the act requirement and the *actus reus* requirement), which, according to Hart, is the orthodox theory of action that has descended to us from legal philosophers such as John Austin, Jeremy Bentham and Oliver Wendell Holmes.[45] Holmes defined action as „a willed muscular contraction, nothing more"[46], Austin (and in the same sense also Bentham) defined it as „a voluntary movement of my body, or a movement which follows a volition" and adds that „bodily movements are the only objects to which the term 'act' can be applied with perfect precision and propriety".[47]

Now, given that criminal laws do not prohibit the performance of bodily movements as such, these writers introduced the idea that the descriptions of actions included in the criminal law do not actually refer to actions, but to descriptions of actions in terms of their consequences and the circumstances in which they were performed. In the words of John Austin:

> „Most of the names which seem to be names of acts, are names of acts, *coupled with certain of their consequences*. For example, if I kill you with a gun or pistol I *shoot* you: And the long train of incidents which are denoted by that brief expression, are considered (or spoken of) as if they constituted an *act* perpetrated by me. In truth, the only parts of the train which are my act or acts are the muscular motions by which I raise the weapon; point it at your head or body, and pull the trigger. These I *will*. The contact of the flint and steel; the ignition of the powder, the flight of the ball towards your body, the wound and subsequent death, with the numberless incidents included in these, are *consequences* of the act which I *will*. I *will* not those consequences, though I may *intend* them."[48]

[43] On this point, cf. Nino 1980, pp. 107 ff. In Anglo-Saxon criminal law, no general doctrine of unlawfulness has been developed, but some authors discuss whether the causes of justification are part of the *actus reus* (in which case one could say that the *actus reus* includes something analogous to the requirement of unlawfulness in Continental law), or whether they are an independent element. On this discussion, cf,. e. g., Moore 1993, pp. 177-183.

[44] Cf. Duff 1993, pp. 74 f.

[45] Hart 1973, p. 95.

[46] Quoted from Moore 1993, p. 78.

[47] Quoted from ibid.

[48] Quoted from Hart 1973, p. 98.

Thus, the norms of the criminal law do not directly refer to actions, but to descriptions of actions. Michael S. Moore, who with solid philosophical arguments recently defended the orthodox theory of action, summarizes it in four theses:

(1) The actions to which the 'act requirement' refers are partially identical with bodily movements.

(2) In fact, the only existing acts are those constituted by bodily movements.

(3) Not every bodily movement is an action; rather, an action must be caused by the will.

(4) The descriptions of actions given in the special part of the criminal law are equivalent to the description of a bodily movement caused by the will of the accused and which brings about a prohibited state of affairs.[49] The canonical form of such descriptions is the following: „In circumstances *C* a basic action *A* causes consequences *E*".[50]

Hart has presented some objections against this theory. For him, to hold that all actions are preceded by a volition, or an internal phase that can adequately be described as a volition, is nothing but fiction. As we can see in the passage by Austin quoted above, the orthodox theory holds that we will the performance of bodily movements. However, Hart points out that this happens only exceptionally: in most actions, we move our muscles without first willing to do so and even without previously thinking about which muscles to move. Our knowledge of the actions we perform is independent of our knowledge of which muscular movements we must make in order to bring them about (a knowledge we are usually not aware of).[51]

To these criticisms, we can add a linguistic objection : the concept of action underlying the language of the criminal law is more complex than the concept which reduces actions to willed bodily movements. The criminal law refers to types of actions such as robbery, murder, manslaughter, or rape; it is perplexing to hear that the only actions that exist are movements of the body and that if we want to know which of these actions (i. e., bodily movements) is, for example, a case of robbery, we must look at the consequences of those movements although they are not part of the action. In other words: we are told that classes of actions are not really classes of actions, but classes of descriptions of actions. As R. A. Duff has remarked, not even advocates of that theory apply it consistently, because once they have thus defined 'action' they seem to abandon the theory, referring naturally to cases of robbery, murder, firing a gun, dangerous conducts, etc., by calling them actions.[52]

3.2. OBJECTIVISM VS. SUBJECTIVISM

[49] Cf. Moore 1993, pp. 44 f.

[50] Ibid. p. 191.

[51] Hart 1973, p. 103.

[52] Cf. Duff 1993, p. 82.

We have seen that the distinction between the act requirement and the *actus reus* requirement led to a debate similar to the one in Continental dogmatics between the advocates of the causal theory of action and their opponents. In both discussions, what is at issue is whether a naturalistic or positivist concept of action provides an adequate object for evaluation and blame. On the other hand, the controversy between the teleological theory and the social theory about whether an approach that emphasizes the agent's intention is more adequate than one that underscores the social relevance of the consequences of an action has its parallel in Anglo-Saxon law in the controversy between *objectivists* and *subjectivists* that, as Richard H. S. Tur says, has dominated the recent intellectual history of the criminal law in England.[53]

The controversy is about the question which aspect – *actus reus* or *mens rea* – has more weight in the determination of criminal responsibility (the question is often formulated in terms of whether or not the subjective aspect – *mens rea* – must encompass all the necessary aspects for an action to be considered an *actus reus*). It seems necessary to give one of these elements greater weight in order to answer questions like the following: Are we responsible for the unforeseeable consequences of our actions? What relevance does knowledge of the legal status of a performed action have? What is the relevance of the motives underlying an action? How should cases of negligence be solved? The objectivist attitude tends to give answers to these questions that come close to what has been called 'objective responsibility', justifying them with clauses such as 'due diligence', 'foreseeability for a reasonable person', 'necessity of compensation', etc.; the subjectivist attitude, in contrast, tends to give greater weight to the mental states that really held, or ceased to hold, in the agent at the moment of performing the action.

The most radical expression of objectivism can be found in Holmes, who „asserted that the law did not consider, and need not consider, in administering punishment what in fact the accused intended but that it imputed to him the intention that an 'ordinary man', equipped with ordinary knowledge, would be taken to have had in acting as the accused did".[54] The general rule that has imposed itself in Anglo-Saxon – as well as in Continental – criminal law is, quite to the contrary, the requirement of intent and foresight of consequences, but that general rule must be qualified in many important cases (for example, concerning the punishment of preterintentional manslaughter).

4. Conclusions

The following conclusions can be drawn from the preceding considerations:

(1) The development of the theory of action in Continental (and also in Anglo-Saxon) criminal law has taken a course parallel to that of the 'philosophers' theory of action'.

(2) The parallels are apparent in the theses defended by each theory as well as in the problems each one of them gives rise to. Thus, Davidson's 'minimizing' theory and

[53] Tur 1993, p. 213.

[54] Hart 1973, p. 38.

the causal theory of criminal dogmatics tend to construct a 'naturalistic' concept of action (that is, an 'uninterpreted' concept ignoring the dimension of meaning). In both theories, this raises problems for the possibility of the evaluation of actions. Von Wright's theory and the teleological theory approach the concept of action focusing on the standpoint of the agent. They can thus account for intentional actions, but not for non-intentional actions. Finally, the theory of Hart and Feinberg and the social theory (as well as Vives's theory of action as meaning), by adopting the point of view of third parties, can account for non-intentional actions for which a theory of imputation seems adequate, but they distort the concept of intentional action (for which it does not seem adequate to speak of the imputation of an action).

(3) Again, all this suggests the possibility to consider the causal theory, the teleological theory, and the social theory (including the theory of action as meaning) not as three competing theories (or groups of theories), but as conceptions pointing toward the three aspects of actions which in the previous chapter I have called 'basic act', 'result-act', and 'consequence-act'.

CHAPTER V

THE DEBATE IN THE PHILOSOPHY OF LANGUAGE

1. Introduction. Good Times for Pragmatics[1]

In an essay published some years ago, Eduardo Bustos wrote that „these are good times for pragmatics, as a theory about actions people perform through language, as well as for those who study pragmatics". He goes on to explain that pragmatics has undergone a drastic change of reputation, from being considered the 'garbage can' or 'wastebasket' for phenomena that could not easily be accomodated in other branches of linguistics, to a respectable discipline practiced by scholars who are organized in associations and publish their own solid periodicals.[2]

According to Bustos, at least the following two reasons for this change can be distinguished:

> „Part of the recent upsurge of the discipline is certainly due to an external factor which, very broadly, can be characterized as the *exhaustion of the structuralist paradigm* that has dominated the century not only in linguistics, but in the entire field of the *symbolic sciences*, as the different disciplines dealing with meaningful human actions are now usually called. But part of the current importance of the discipline is also due to an internal factor which is that it has succeeded in elaborating a system of notions and concepts for the analysis of some of the most intractable and intriguing aspects of human communication through language."[3]

Bustos proposes a definition of pragmatics that is of great interest for a general theory of action: in his view, „pragmatics deals with the way how we *ascribe meaning to our actions* when we perform them, *or to the actions of others* when we understand them".[4] Seen in this light, pragmatics encompasses linguistic pragmatics, but at the same time it seems to be a branch of the theory of human action. The connexion between the philosophy of language and the theory of action is also emphasized by John Searle when he states that „a theory of language is part of a theory of action, simply because speaking is a rule-governed form of behavior".[5]

[1] Some writers distinguish between 'philosophy of language' and 'linguistic philosophy'. According to John Searle, for instance, the former is the study of certain general features of language whereas the latter is a method for the solution of philosophical problems concerning the study of ordinary language. Cf. Searle 1969, p. 4. Here, we will be dealing with the philosophy of language in Searle's sense.

[2] Bustos 1997, p. 264.

[3] Ibid. p. 265.

[4] Ibid. p. 294.

[5] Searle 1969, p. 17.

The greatest merit of linguistic pragmatics is, according to Bustos, that it has rescued meaning from the hands of language and returned it to man, replacing the „model of language as a code" by an „inferential model of language":

„One of the fundamental assumptions on which the inferential model is based is of a negative or critical nature: the processes of codification and decodification play no significant role in the description and explanation of linguistic communication [...] What is fundamental is the operation of *inference* which consists essentially in the production or reception of an information on the basis of a set of previous informations [...] The central axis of a pragmatic explanation of the production of meaning is an inference about *communicative intentions*: the speaker infers the adequate means for the expression of his communicative intentions, given his knowledge of the situation, and the audience infers the communicative intention of the speaker, i. e. what he has wanted to say, from what the speaker has done."[6]

In the next pages, we will look at how this process has come about. Given the complexity and sheer number of works that could be considered as belonging to linguistic pragmatics in a wide sense, I will only refer to those regarded as major breakthroughs in the development of that discipline.

2. Language Games (Wittgenstein)[7]

The first step in the turn towards a pragmatic conception of meaning can be found in the second Wittgenstein, in texts such as *Philosophical Investigations*, the *Blue Book*, or the *Brown Book*. In his later works (and against the theses he once held in the *Tractatus*), Wittgenstein points out that ordinary language is much richer than logic and that the latter therefore cannot give a full account of the former (nor of reality). He adds that this complexity of ordinary language implies that there is nothing that all linguistic phenomena have in common, which is why there can be no general theory of them. We use the term 'language' to refer to a great number of phenomena because these phenomena are interrelated in multiple different ways, and it is this web of relations, rather than any property they all have in common, that allows us to say that they all 'belong' to language.

As is well-known, Wittgenstein compares linguistic phenomena to games: just like games, these phenomena have a certain 'family resemblance', and, just as with games, it is impossible to give a definition that encompasses them all. Wittgenstein offers a long list of 'linguistic games':

„Giving orders, and obeying them –
Describing the appearance of an object, or giving its measurements –
Constructing an object from a description (a drawing) –
Reporting an event –
Speculating about an event –
Forming and testing a hypothesis –
Presenting the results of an experiment in tables and diagrams –

[6] Bustos 1997, p. 267.

[7] In this section, I rely heavily on Hierro S. Pescador 1982, esp. the section on 'Meaning and use in the second Wittgenstein'.

Making up a story; and reading it –
Play-acting –
Singing catches –
Guessing riddles –
Making a joke; telling it –
Solving a problem in practical arithmetic –
Translating from one language into another –
Asking, thanking, cursing, greeting, praying.“[8]

Each of these language games constitutes a different use of language. We can understand the examples as cases of situations in which we do something by using language (where 'using language' can mean making an utterance, as in the case of giving orders, as well as receiving one, as in the case of obeying orders). Besides, Wittgenstein seems to suggest that there is no limit to the uses of language because they are constantly changing. After all, „For a *large* class of cases– though not for all – in which we employ the word 'meaning' it can be defined thus: the meaning of a word is its use in the language“.[9]

This last assertion is what contains the impulse for a pragmatic theory of language. The conception of language sketched by the second Wittgenstein can be summarized in the following points:[10]

(a) Language is a tool, or a set of tools: words, concepts, are tools for playing an immense variety of linguistic games.

(b) What is relevant for the determination of meaning is the use we make of these tools, and to determine this, it is not enough to look exclusively at the tool (which is what the earlier theory of meaning, including that of the first Wittgenstein, is thought to have done); one must also take into account the actions that accompany the utterance of words, because speaking a language is part of a more complex activity, of a form of life.

(c) An analysis of language from this perspective reveals that the use of words in language, in language games, is subject to rules. And these rules allow us to speak of a correct or incorrect use of language and also to predict the linguistic conduct of others.

(d) All that does not mean that the rules must always be perfectly well defined or that they cover all possible cases.

The panorama resulting from this conception of language is at the same time attractive and confusing. It is attractive because it enables us to account for the meaning of expressions that are not descriptive – something that had been impossible with previous conceptions which were focused on the meaning of propositions (that is why Austin spoke of the 'descriptive fallacy'). And it is confusing because Wittgenstein does not provide an ordered classification of the different uses of language and even seems to

[8] Wittgenstein 1958, § 23.

[9] Ibid. § 43.

[10] Cf. Hierro S. Pescador 1982, p. 117.

suggest that such a classification is impossible. Hence, it seems that the task of explaining language is restricted to a mere casuistic description of some of its uses.

Starting from Wittgenstein's observations, pragmatics has in the meantime developed into various directions. Here, however, I will look only at two lines of the development of the conception of meaning as the use of language, namely: the intentional theory of meaning of H. P. Grice, and the speech-act theory fundamentally elaborated by J. L. Austin and John Searle.

3. An Intentional Theory of Meaning (H. P. Grice)

3.1. THE RECONSTRUCTION OF SEMANTIC CONCEPTS FROM PRAGMATIC CONCEPTS

One of the roads opened up by the conception that the meaning of an expression depends on its use is that of analyzing the intentions with which speakers utter such expressions and on that basis determine the conditions that must hold for the expression to be meaningful. If the meaning of an expression depends on its use, and that – being an action: the playing of a language game –, in turn, depends on the intention of the speaker (who can decide how to use linguistic tools, in accordance with the respective purpose), it seems that the meaning of an expression depends on the intention of the speaker. To make intentions central for the explanation of meaning is a totally different strategy for the determination of the meaning of an expression or utterance: instead of asking about the meaning of each and every word and regarding the meaning of an utterance as a function of the meaning of each of its components, the task now is to find out what the speaker intended with the utterance of a particular expression at a certain moment and in a certain context, i. e., what he meant to say, and to extract the 'usual' or 'permanent' meaning of that utterance from that intention. In other words, we are here dealing with the construction of semantic notions from pragmatic notions.

This is what – on a high technical level – H. P. Grice has proposed in several papers, among them especially 'Meaning' (1948), 'Utterer's Meaning and Intentions' (1967), and 'Utterer's Meaning, Sentence-Meaning and Word-Meaning' (1967). Grice's starting point is the concept of *utterer's meaning* or *occasion-meaning*, which he explains as the intention of the speaker to bring about, or cause, a certain effect in the audience (that is why the theory has also been known, somewhat inappropriately,[11] as the causal theory of meaning). Thus, according to a first definition, to state that an utterer means something with his words is equivalent to saying that the utterer has the intention to bring about, or cause, a reaction or response in the audience.[12] Now, according to Grice, that primary intention must be accompanied by some secondary or complementary intentions: the wish that the audience recognize the speaker's intention, and the wish that this recognition will lead it to respond. In Grice's own words:

[11] Cf. below, in this subsection.

[12] Grice 1989b, p. 217.

„*A* must intend to induce by *x* a belief in an audience, and he must also intend his utterance to be recognized as so intended. But these intentions are not independent; the recognition is intended by *A* to play its part in inducing the belief [...]“[13]

If these secondary or complementary intentions are integrated into the definition of the utterer's meaning or occasion-meaning of an utterance, we get the following: That an utterer *U* wants to say something to an audience *A* by an utterance *u* is true if and only if *U* utters *u* with the triple intention that:

(1) *A* come up with a particular response *r*;
(2) *A* recognize that intention of *U*; and
(3) that recognition should be, at least partly, the reason why *A* responds with *r*.[14]

What are the possible responses of the audience? Grice deals with two kinds of responses and the corresponding intentions to bring them about (it must be underscored that what is essential for an utterance to have meaning is not that the response actually comes about, but that the utterer intends to provoke it): on the one hand, he analyzes descriptive utterances where the utterer has the intention of inducing a certain belief in the hearer; on the other, he analyzes directive or normative utterances where the speaker intends the hearer to do something (in Grice's treatment, it is not sufficiently clear whether he thinks that the two types of utterances are an exhaustive classification). Later, in response to some criticisms, Grice qualifies both intentions: since the speaker often is not trying to convince the hearer, but simply to let him know that he (the speaker) has a certain belief, the effect the speaker intends to bring about with descriptive utterances must be that the hearer thinks that the speaker believes something; for reasons of symmetry, what the speaker intends in the case of normative utterances is not that the hearer does something, but that he has the intention of doing it.

The utterer's meaning or occasion-meaning is the meaning of 'utterance-tokens', i. e., of statements uttered by a speaker at a certain time and place. Starting from this truly pragmatic notion, Grice attempts to define the meaning of 'utterance-types' (which is, in fact, a traditionally semantic notion).[15] This is the meaning we refer to in saying things like 'Expression *x* means ...' (instead of 'The utterer meant that ...'). Grice calls this the *timeless meaning*, which he defines as follows (I follow the simplified version of José Hierro):

„For an utterer *U*, utterance-type *x* means something if and only if the following *procedure* is part of *U*'s *repertoire*: that he utters a token of expression *x* whenever he intends the hearer to come up with a certain response.“[16]

[13] Ibid. p. 219.

[14] Grice 1989a, p. 92. Later, Grice increases the complexity of that definition in response to objections by his critics, but we do not need to go into the details here.

[15] The distinction between utterance-type and utterance-token is equivalent, on the level of language, to the distinction presented in Chapter I, sect. 1, between generic action (act-type) and individual action (act-token).

[16] Hierro S. Pescador 1982, p. 182 (emphasis added).

Thus, the utterance-token 'It is raining' means something for a speaker insofar as he will rely on the procedure of uttering that statement whenever he wishes to produce in the hearer the response of attributing to him (the speaker) the belief that it is raining.[17] The above definition refers exclusively to the timeless meaning of an utterance for a speaker, but not for a language. In order to construct the concept of *timeless meaning in a language*, Grice makes use of a generalization:

„For a community *C*, utterance-type *x* means something if and only if some (many?) members of *C* have in their repertoires the procedure of uttering a token of *x* whenever they have the intention to bring about a certain response in the hearer, where the retention of that procedure is conditional on the fact that at least some (other) members of *C* have, or have had, this procedure in their repertoires.“.[18]

Here, I'm afraid, we need to introduce yet another notion, to wit, that of the *applied timeless meaning* of an utterance-type, i. e., the meaning we have in mind when an expression has several timeless meanings and we say 'In this case, expression *x* means ...'. Obviously, this sense of 'meaning' occupies an intermediate position between timeless meaning and occasion-meaning (with which it can coincide), and its definition can be obtained on the basis of the definition of timeless meaning, by adding a reference to certain specific elements of the speech act: For an utterer *U*, expression *p* means *x* in situation *S* if and only if uttering *p* in situation *S* is a procedure from the repertoire of *U* for bringing about the corresponding response in the hearer (in turn, this definition needs to be adapted to render the applied timeless meaning in a language).

3.2. THE ROLE OF CONVENTIONS IN THE DETERMINATION OF MEANING

The main objection against the program of reconstructing semantic notions from pragmatic notions pursued by Grice has been that he relies too much on the defining capacity of the utterer's intention, thereby ignoring the conventional nature of language.[19] However, it would be unfair to think that Grice has not taken conventions into account at all in dealing with the question of meaning (at least in his last works on that subject), although he has done so insufficiently.

To see the role of conventions and their treatment by Grice, let us look at a – not very unlikely – example: Suppose I have decided to 'conquer' a girlfriend with whom I am desperately in love. A good friend who is an expert in this field recommends that I try to make her laugh, as part of an elaborate plan which he explains to me in all detail. When the time has come – you may think of a nice little pub and a few drinks on the table – I decide to make my girlfriend laugh by telling her a joke, but I am so bad at it

[17] Here is another example that illustrates the notion of procedure: „Two drivers meet at an intersection, and one of them asks the other what route he must take to get to a certain place. Now, the other one waves his left arm out of the window of his car in a certain way in order to tell him to follow him. Obviously, in such a case we can say that the gesture means what in words we would express as 'Follow me!'. The driver who was asked has a procedure by which to tell the other party to follow him: the procedure is to put his left arm through the window and wave it in a certain manner“. Acero/Bustos/Quesada 1982, p. 178.

[18] Hierro S. Pescador 1982, p. 183; cf. also Grice 1971, 62.

[19] Searle 1969; Hierro S. Pescador 1982, pp. 184 ff.

that it is precisely the fact of my trying to make her laugh with so little chances of success which does make her laugh. Here, Grice's conditions for saying that my utterance had meaning are satisfied: I have the intention of making her laugh, and I want her to laugh because she recognizes my intention to make her laugh; she in fact does recognize my intention and laughs because she recognizes it (although she does not laugh because she thinks my joke is funny). And yet, would we say that these conditions are sufficient to say that my utterance had meaning? Note that there is a certain sense in which my utterance may not be meaningful: It is possible that my natural nervousness in such circumstances prevented me from counting the joke in a minimally coherent manner and that it was therefore incomprehensible. Moreover, it is possible that I have not even been able to finish telling the joke (for example, I may have suffered an attack of nervous coughing), despite of which she – with the condescending superiority some women display in such situations – has recognized my intention to make her laugh, and laughs.

Grice apparently wants to exclude such cases from the definition of meaning. To that end, he says that the recognition of the utterer's intention by the hearer must be „at least part of his reason for producing *r* (the response), and not merely the *cause* of his producing *r*".[20] He does not explain this very clearly, but it seems that we can understand this requirement in the sense that between the hearer's response and his recognition of the utterer's intention there must exist not a causal, but a conventional relationship. If we interpret Grice in this way, we find that there must be some conventional regularity between our utterances and a hearer's response. In the example of the joke, there is no conventional regularity between my stammering and my friend's laughing, which is why the example does not fall under Grice's definition of occasion-meaning. But Grice does not say what that regularity consists of. When we go from the notion of occasion-meaning to that of timeless meaning or applied timeless meaning, the conventional element reappears in the ideas of procedure and repertoire. Grice maintains that to have a linguistic procedure is to 'have the equipment' for using a linguistic expression, but again he does not elaborate on this idea.

In summary, Grice is well aware of the fact that conventions must be introduced in the explication of (occasional, timeless and applied timeless) meaning, but he leaves this part of the definition of meaning in the dark. The fact that he has not developed the role of conventions as determinants of meaning makes him give too much weight to intentions. That is the core of John Searle's critique which I will present next.

3.3. SEARLE'S CRITIQUE OF THE CONCEPTION OF GRICE

Once we pay due attention to the role of rules and conventions in language, we will find that a speaker's intentions (what Grice calls 'utterer's meaning') do not completely determine the 'occasion-meaning' of an utterance. To show this, John Searle has used the following example:

„Suppose that I am an American soldier in the Second World War and that I am captured by Italian troops. And suppose also that I wish to get these troops to believe that I am a German officer in order to get them to

[20] Grice 1989a, p. 92.

release me. What I would like to do is to tell them in German or Italian that I am a German officer. But let us suppose I don't know enough German or Italian to do that. So I, as it were, attempt to put on a show of telling them that I am a German officer by reciting those few bits of German that I know, trusting that they don't know enough German to see through my plan. Let us suppose I know only one line of German, which I remember from a poem I had to memorize in a high-school German course. Therefore I, a captured American, address my Italian captors with the following sentence: 'Kennst Du das Land, wo die Zitronen blühen?'"[21]

The 'normal' meaning of that sentence is not 'I'm a German soldier', but 'Do you know the country where the lemon-trees bloom?'; but in Searle's example that sentence is used to make the Italians believe that the speaker is trying to tell them that he is a German soldier, and he might even succeed in making them believe just that – after all, who else would be speaking German in that region? In this example, the intention of the speaker is to induce a certain belief in his audience, and to induce it through the recognition of the audience that this is his intention. Now, would we say that the occasion-meaning of the utterance '*Kennst Du das Land, wo die Zitronen blühen?*' in this case is not 'Do you know the country where the lemon-trees bloom?' but 'I am a German soldier'? Searle denies this (despite the belief induced in the Italian soldiers), which shows, in his view, that what the utterance in fact means (the occasion-meaning of the sentence) does not entirely depend on what the speaker wants to make believe (the utterer's meaning). And Searle seems to suggest more, namely that it would not even make sense to say that the speaker *meant to say* that he is a German soldier (although he meant to *make them believe* it), since he knew very well that the words conventionally mean something else. Thus, the meaning of our utterances depends not only on intention and context; it is also a function of what the utterances conventionally mean.[22] In contrast, one of the consequences apparently deriving from Grice's theory is that, although he claims to deny it, in the right context any utterance can be used to say anything at all.

Note, however, that this critique of Grice's view must not be understood as a rejection of the idea that intentions have an important function as determinants of meaning. As Luis M. Valdés Villanueva has remarked, intentions allow us to separate cases of natural meaning (as when we say that some clouds in the sky 'mean' that it is likely that it will rain) from cases of non-natural meaning (as with any linguistic utterance), and that they have an important theoretical role because they allow us to define 'meaning' in a non-circular way (in terms of intentions and rules).[23] All the critique wants to clarify is that intentions are not alone with that task[24] and that – as we will see later – perhaps the most relevant are not intentions to bring about perlocutionary effects, but other kinds of effects. This last assertion, as well as the function of conventions as determinants of meaning, can be more easily understood if we follow a current of lingu-

[21] Searle 1969, p. 44; 1971, pp. 45 f.

[22] Searle 1969, p. 45.

[23] Valdés Villanueva 1978, p. 191.

[24] According to Valdés Villanueva, there are three kinds of determinants of meaning: rules and conventions, intentions, and context.

istic pragmatics which was developed at about the same time, but independently of the one followed by Grice, to wit, the theory of speech acts.[25]

4. How To Do Things With Words (J. L. Austin)

4.1. 'CONSTATIVE UTTERANCES' AND 'PERFORMATIVE UTTERANCES'

John L. Austin is probably the philosopher who has dedicated himself more extensively and profoundly than any other to the analysis of ordinary language, either as a means for reaching a better understanding of language as such or as a way of approaching many problems of philosophy and other areas of knowledge (thus, for example, his essay 'A Plea for Excuses' is an analysis of the concept of action through ordinary language).

Austin's main contribution to the theory of meaning is his analysis of speech acts. His starting point is the investigation of the differences between two types of utterances: *performative utterances* and *constative utterances*,[26] intended as a contribution to the clarification of the possible uses of language.

Although he had already hinted at the distinction in previous works,[27] Austin treats it more deeply in *How To Do Things With Words*. There, he begins by pointing out that the differences between the two types of utterances are fundamentally of two kinds: „(1) the performative should be *doing* something as opposed to *just* saying something; and (2) the performative is happy or unhappy [i. e., successful or unsuccessful; DGL] as opposed to true or false".[28] Examples of performatives are 'I promise ...', 'Yes, I do' (in the marriage ceremony), 'I baptize you ...', 'I advise you to ...', 'I bet you ...', 'I bequeath you my watch', etc.

The success or failure of a performative depends on whether or not certain conditions are satisfied:

> „(A.1) There must exist an accepted conventional procedure having a certain conventional effect, that procedure must include the uttering of certain words by certain persons in certain circumstances, and further,
> (A.2) the particular persons and circumstances in a given case must be appropriate for the invocation of the particular procedure invoked.
> (B.1) The procedure must be executed by all participants both correctly and
> (B.2) completely.
> (Γ.1) Where, as often, the procedure is designed for use by persons having certain thoughts or feelings, or for the inauguration of certain consequential conduct on the part of any participant, then a person participating in and so invoking the procedure must in fact have those thoughts or feelings, and the participants must intend so to conduct themselves, and further

[25] As we have seen, when Wittgenstein initiated the turn towards pragmatics, he himself had emphasized the importance of rules for the determination of the correctness or incorrectness of our use of language.

[26] Austin introduces the expression 'constative', which is a neologism in English, in order to avoid calling them 'descriptive', since „Not all true or false statements are descriptions"; Austin 1976, p. 3.

[27] Austin 1979b.

[28] Austin 1976, 133; emphasis added.

(Γ.2) must actually so conduct themselves subsequently."[29]

If any one of these conditions is violated, different kinds of „infelicities" befall the performative. Insatisfaction of A.1, A.2, B.1, or B.2 lead to the performative not being achieved at all, whereas insatisfaction of Γ.1 or Γ.2 leads to insincere acts which, though not void of effect, amount to something like an „abuse" of a procedure.[30]

However, once the distinction between performatives and constatives has thus been drawn, we can see that throughout the different lectures collected in *How To Do Things With Words* Austin is disturbed by growing doubts. On the one hand, it is difficult for him to provide criteria for upholding the distinctions beyond those already mentioned, i. e., that *(1)* performatives do something rather than merely say something, and *(2)* that they are not true or false, but happy or unhappy (for example, he finds no standard grammatical form that is exclusive to performatives). On the other, the two criteria he does have turn out to be insufficient in many cases. Thus, there are cases of apparent performatives which are related to the categories of truth or falsehood, such as 'I conclude that *p*', 'I predict that *p*', or 'I argue that *p*', as well as cases of apparent constatives for which the categories 'happy' (or successful) or 'unhappy' (unsuccessful) seem more appropriate than those of 'true' or 'false' (for example, the sentence 'The King of France is bald' could be considered a void statement in the same sense as when I say that I bequeath my watch to someone without having a watch).

But the most disturbing doubt is the one that arises when we come to the distinction between implicit and explicit performatives. Explicit performatives contain a verb which explicitly mentions the action being performed with the utterance. Thus, the following utterances are explicit performatives:

> *(1)* 'I *advise* you to think it over carefully.'
> *(2)* 'I *promise* you that I will come.'

And the following are implicit performatives:

> *(1')* 'Think it over carefully.'
> *(2')* 'I will come.'

The problem appears when we wonder about statements such as *(3)* 'I inform you that he promises that he will come', or *(3')* 'He promises that he will come'. These statements seem to be at the same time constative and performative: constative, because they are both true or false; and performative, because with both the action of informing someone is performed (I can perform the action of informing someone either by saying 'I inform you that he promises that he will come' or simply by saying 'He promises that he will come'; the only difference is that *(3)* seems to be an explicit and *(3')* an implicit performative).[31]

29 Ibid. pp. 14 f.

30 Ibid. p. 16.

31 Ibid. pp. 133 ff.

All this seems to lead us to the conclusion that uttering, describing or stating are actions just like promising, advising, or betting, and thus the distinction between performatives and constatives dissolves and the investigation is left at best with a distinction between explicit and implicit performatives, or with an analysis of performative verbs. In the final pages of his book and in other works, Austin acknowledges that the distinction between constative and performative utterances „is considerably weakened and indeed breaks down“.[32]

4.2. 'LOCUTIONARY ACTS', 'ILLOCUTIONARY ACTS', AND 'PERLOCUTIONARY ACTS'

But let us go back to the beginning for a moment. We have seen that Austin's initial purpose was to distinguish between merely saying something and doing something by saying something. His original idea was that describing, stating and informing are on the level of 'merely saying', but in the course of his analysis he ends up showing that to say something is *always* (even with descriptive statements) also doing something more (like describing). Now, once we have come to that conclusion we can ask in what sense and in what way *saying* something is doing something else, and what connection there is between the two levels of meaning. About halfway through *How To Do Things With Words*, Austin takes this new direction and offers one of the most important distinctions in the philosophy of language. In his own words, it involves the following:

„We first distinguished a group of things we do in saying something, which together we summed up by saying we perform a *locutionary act*, which is roughly equivalent to uttering a certain sentence with a certain sense and reference, which again is roughly equivalent to 'meaning' in the traditional sense. Second, we said that we also perfom *illocutionary acts* such as informing, ordering, warning, undertaking, &c., i. e., utterances which have a certain (conventional) force. Thirdly, we may also perform *perlocutionary acts*: what we bring about or achieve *by* saying something, such as convincing, persuading, deterring, and even, say, surprising or misleading.“[33]

In what follows, I will try to systematize some assertions about these kinds of acts that are somewhat dispersed in Austin's book:

(1) On locutionary acts

a) A locutionary act is an act on the level of merely 'saying something'.

b) A locutionary act is composed of three other 'acts' or aspects (that is, things we do when uttering a locution): a *phonetic act*, consisting in the uttering of certain sounds; a *phatic act*, consisting in the uttering of those sounds as belonging to a vocabulary and being regulated by a grammar; and a *rhetic act*, consisting in uttering those sounds with a more or less fixed sense and reference.

c) The meaning of an utterance, in the 'traditional sense' of meaning (as sense and reference), lies in the *rhetic act*.

[32] Austin 1979c, p. 251.

[33] Austin 1976, p. 109.

d) These three 'acts' can be seen as descriptions of increasing complexity of one and the same act: If we ignore sense and reference, what is left is the utterance of certain sounds conforming to a grammar, but without meaning (as when someone issues an utterance the meaning of which he does not know). And if we ignore conformity to a grammar, we are left with an utterance of mere sounds.

e) Locutionary acts depend on conventions.[34]

(2) On illocutionary acts

a) The illocutionary act is not merely the act of saying something, but consists in what we are doing in saying something, i. e., in performing an illocutionary act.

b) The difference between the two types of acts can be illustrated with examples like the following: The statement 'He said to me: >You must study<' refers to a locutionary act, whereas the statement 'He advised me to study' refers to an illocutionary act (that is, to what he does by issuing that utterance). Austin offers the following example:

> „For example, it might be perfectly possible, with regard to an utterance, say 'It is going to charge', to make entirely plain 'what we are saying' in issuing the utterance, in all the senses so far distinguished [i. e., meaning as sense and reference; DGL], and yet not at all to have cleared up whether or not in issuing the utterance I was performing the act of *warning* or not. It may be perfectly clear what I mean by 'It is going to charge' or 'Shut the door', but not clear whether it is meant as a statement or warning, &c."[35]

c) While meaning, in its literal sense that is more or less equivalent to sense and reference, depends on the locutionary act (more precisely, on the rhetic act), there is another dimension, the *illocutionary force*, related to an illocutionary act. An utterance such as 'Think it over carefully' can have different illocutionary forces: it may be a request, an advice, an order, etc. Depending on the illocutionary force of an utterance, we can speak of an illocutionary act of 'requesting', 'advising', 'ordering', etc. For a complete understanding of an utterance, both its meaning and its illocutionary force must be understood.

d) Whenever I perform a locutionary act, I perform *eo ipso* an illocutionary act. But illocutionary acts must not be regarded as causal consequences of locutionary acts; rather, they are conventional effects. The relation between a locutionary act and an illocutionary act is a conventional relation, depending on the satisfaction of certain conditions.

e) Because of such conventions, illocutionary acts are linked to the production of effects in several senses:

e.1, For an illocutionary act to come about, there must be a certain effect on the audience: „Generally the effect amounts to bringing about the understanding of the

[34] Austin (ibid. p. 107) says this only in passing: „the illocutionary act and even the locutionary act too involve conventions"; but it is an important point because it implies that there are two kinds of conventions related to meaning: those linked to meaning as sense and reference, and those linked to illocutionary force.

[35] Austin 1976, p. 98.

meaning and of the force of the locution. So the performance of an illocutionary act involves the securing of *uptake*."[36]

e.2, Illocutionary acts sometimes have characteristic effects. For example, to say „'I name this ship the *Queen Elizabeth'* has the effect of naming or christening the ship" and this is „distinguished from producing consequences in the sense of bringing about states of affairs in the 'normal' way, i. e. changes in the natural course of events"[37] (with this qualification, Austin wants to distinguish this kind of 'illocutionary effects' from the consequences implied in 'perlocutionary acts').

e.3, Some illocutionary acts 'require', because of a convention, a certain characteristic response from the hearer (as in the case of 'asking') or from the speaker himself (as in the case of 'promising'). Austin himself, however, seems unsure whether such responses should be regarded as effects of an illocutionary act or as part of a perlocutionary act.[38]

(3) On perlocutionary acts

a) „Saying something", i. e., performing a locutionary act, and with it an illocutionary act, „will often [...] produce certain consequential effects upon the feelings, thoughts, or actions of the audience, or of the speaker, or of other persons".[39] In that case, the act of the person issuing the utterance can be described by individuating it (this is not Austin's expression, but it reflects his thinking) on the basis of that consequence, mentioning only marginally, or not at all, the kind of locutionary and illocutionary acts performed. The act thus individuated is a perlocutionary act.

b) Perlocutionary acts, therefore, are (or, more precisely: are individuated with a view towards) consequences of illocutionary acts, that is, of what is being done in saying something (as we have already seen, it is not easy to distinguish between the consequential effects of illocutionary acts which give rise to perlocutionary acts and those which don't).

c) The relationship between illocutionary acts and perlocutionary acts is not a conventional relationship: „perlocutionary acts are not conventional, though conventional acts may be made use of in order to bring off the perlocutionary act".[40] That illocutionary acts are conventional whereas perlocutionary acts are not can be seen in the fact that the former may be performed through performative utterances (such as 'I warn you ...', 'I promise you ...', 'I order you to ...', 'I inform you that ...', etc.), whereas the latter cannot (we cannot say 'I convince you that ...', 'I impress you with ...', 'I disappoint you with ...', etc.).

[36] Ibid. p. 117. This statement, however, contradicts Austin's previous assertion that a locutionary act by itself brings about an illocutionary act. This obscurity in Austin raises the question whether when the illocutionary force of an utterance is not understood, this is a failure on the locutionary or on the illocutionary level. For a discussion of this problem, cf. Valdés Villanueva 1978.

[37] Austin 1976, 117.

[38] Ibid. pp. 117 f.

[39] Ibid. p. 101.

[40] Ibid. p. 122.

d) The fact that they can be produced by non-locutionary means is characteristic of perlocutionary effects (for example, one can threaten someone merely „by swinging a stick“[41]).

e) We must distinguish between actions that have a *perlocutionary object* and actions that merely bring about a *perlocutionary sequel*.[42] Austin does not clarify the distinction, but his examples seem to imply that a perlocutionary object is an effect that is sought intentionally, whereas a 'sequel' is an unintended effect. Austin illustrates the distinction with the example that an act intended to alert someone may have the effect of merely alarming him.[43]

(4) On the three types of acts together

a) Since all three types of acts are acts, they are all subject to the problems of a general theory of action. Thus, the speaker might want to produce an effect and fail (we then speak of an attempt to perform the act), or an effect may be produced that was not intended (we then speak of unintended actions).[44]

b) If we link these three types of actions to the notion of *use of language*, we find that, as this expression is used by many philosophers, it contains an ambiguity, because it may refer to the use of language in order to perform a locutionary act, or to perform an illocutionary act, or to perform a perlocutionary act.

c) „Furthermore, in general the locutionary act as much as the illocutionary is an abstraction only: every genuine speech act is both.“[45] And Austin would surely say the same of perlocutionary acts, in case such an act is performed (because, as we have seen, an illocutionary act must not necessarily amount to a perlocutionary act).

Now, how can all these considerations be applied to our initial question about the distinction between performatives and constatives? As we have seen, all utterances have a locutionary and an illocutionary use (and may also have a perlocutionary use); their illocutionary use corresponds to the previous notion of a performative. Thus, in some sense, all utterances are, explicitly or implicitly, performatives.[46] This leads Austin to offer a classification of different illocutionary forces, taking as a guideline a classification of performative verbs, that is, verbs that serve to utter explicit performatives. Austin distinguishes the following five classes:

1. *Verdictive* verbs, which serve to utter verdicts, estimations, evaluations, etc. Verbs of this kind are, for instance, 'to acquit', 'to convict', 'to value', 'to diagnose', 'to estimate'.

41 Ibid. p. 119.

42 Ibid. p. 118.

43 Ibid.

44 Ibid. p. 106.

45 Ibid. p. 147.

46 Cf. Hierro S. Pescador 1982, p. 156.

2. *Exercitive* verbs, which serve for exercising „powers, rights, or influence", such as „appointing, voting, ordering, urging, advising, warning, &c.".[47]

3. *Commissive* verbs, which serve for committing oneself more or less strongly to an action. Austin notes that besides promises this category contains weaker forms of commitment, such as declarations of intent or taking a side. Verbs of this kind are 'to promise', 'to plan', 'to agree', 'to have the intention', 'to oppose', 'to support', etc.

4. *Behabitive* verbs, which constitute, Austin says, „a very miscellaneous group, and have to do with attitudes and *social behaviour*. Examples are apologizing, congratulating, commending, condoling, cursing, and challenging".[48]

5. *Expositive* verbs, which „make plain how our utterances fit into the course of an argument or conversation",[49] such as 'to argue', 'to reply', 'to postulate', 'to explain', 'to refer to', 'to take back', 'to object', etc.

It is widely held that this classification is one of the weakest points in Austin's scheme (though he himself is aware of that and presents it merely as a tentative proposal). As José Hierro has remarked, its defects[50] undoubtedly derive from the fact that it is not a classification of speech acts (in the sense of illocutionary acts[51]), but of illocutionary verbs.

Taking up the task left by Austin, John Searle has tried to give a new 'turn of the screw' to the theory of speech acts.

5. An Integrative Theory of Speech Acts (J. Searle)

5.1. INTRODUCTION

John Searle's speech-act theory, as elaborated mainly in his book *Speech Acts* (1969) and the two essays 'What Is a Speech Act?' (1971) and 'A Taxonomy of Illocutionary Acts' (1979), integrates the most interesting contributions of the second Wittgenstein (the idea that language is an activity regulated by rules), Grice (the importance of intentions for the distinction between natural and non-natural meaning and for the determination of the latter), and Austin (from whom Searle adopts part of the distinction of three types of speech acts as well as the need for a classification of illocutionary acts). But besides these pragmatic conceptions of language, Searle also considers the 'semantic' tradition represented by Frege and the first Wittgenstein, and holds that the two

[47] Austin 1976, p. 151.

[48] Ibid. p. 152.

[49] Ibid.

[50] Cf. below, sect. 5.3.

[51] There is a certain, rather disturbing, ambiguity in the term 'speech act', because sometimes it is used to refer to any kind of linguistic act considered as a whole, and sometimes it is used to refer to each one of the aspects of a speech act as such (thus, sometimes it is said that the locutionary act, the illocutionary act and the perlocutionary act are three kinds of speech acts), and still other times it is used to refer exclusively to illocutionary acts.

traditions are not inconsistent, but merely different and complementary approaches.[52] The complementarity becomes evident in the realm of speech acts: A definition of the meaning of a sentence must take into account the fact that the sentence might be used (with its literal meaning) to perform a particular speech act; and a definition of a speech act must take into account that its performance requires the utterance, in a certain context, of a sentence with a literal meaning.[53] This takes us to a point we have already seen: what a speaker intends to say with a sentence at some specific moment is a function – among other things – of what the sentence means.

Sometimes, Searle's work has been interpreted as a follow-up on Austin (which, as I have said, to some extent is true); but that must not obscure the fact that there are also important differences between the two. One of the most relevant we find in the analysis of the elements of speech acts. Austin's distinction between locutionary, illocutionary, and perlocutionary acts is partially criticized by Searle. Specifically, Searle – who refers to those elements of speech acts in general as „kinds of speech acts"[54] – criticizes the distinction between locutionary and illocutionary acts, and he does so for several reasons. First of all, Searle holds that *saying* is just another (the most general) illocutionary act and that, therefore, locutionary acts (which consist in *saying* something) can be reduced to that illocutionary act. Secondly, Searle holds that in the case of explicit performatives (such as 'I beg you to listen to me'), the meaning of the words itself determines the illocutionary force (that it is a case of 'begging') and, therefore, in such cases we cannot distinguish the rhetic aspect (linked to the locutionary act) from the illocutionary aspect.

Searle thus prefers to distinguish the following kinds of speech acts: *utterance acts* (uttering words), *propositional acts* (referring and predicating), *illocutionary acts*, and (though on a different level) *perlocutionary acts*.[55] Here, I will not be concerned with propositional acts, but only with the treatment Searle gives to illocutionary acts.

5.2. RULES AND SPEECH ACTS. THE STRUCTURE OF ILLOCUTIONARY ACTS

5.2.1. One of the great merits of speech-act theory is that it pays attention to rules in language. For Searle, to speak a language is a way of conduct that is regulated by rules. This assertion must be qualified with three considerations:

(a) The first consideration is that we must distinguish between linguistic *rules* and linguistic *conventions*. When he says that language is a rule-guided activity, Searle means to say something more than the simple assertion that to speak Spanish requires to follow one convention, and to speak English requires to follow another. Searle is aware of the fact that every particular language depends on a convention; but what he wants to

[52] Searle 1969, pp. 18 f.

[53] Ibid. pp. 17 f.

[54] Ibid. pp. 22 ff.

[55] Ibid. pp. 23 ff. Once perlocutionary acts have been distinguished, they are usually considered not to be of interest for a theory of language.

underscore is the fact that language (not French, or English, or Russian, but language as such) is also a conventional activity, that to perform an illocutionary act (in whatever language) is something we can do only because there are certain rules (shared by particular languages) which 'constitute' such illocutionary acts. Searle reserves the term 'rule' for these conventions shared by all particular languages (the specific conventions of particular languages he simply calls 'conventions'). That is what he wants to say in the following passage:

„Different human languages, to the extent they are inter-translatable, can be regarded as different conventional realizations *of the same underlying rules*. The fact that in French one can make a promise by saying 'je promets' and in English one can make it by saying 'I promise' is a matter of convention. But the fact that an utterance of a promising device (under appropriate conditions) counts as the undertaking of an obligation is a matter of rules and not a matter of the conventions of French or English.“[56]

(b) The second consideration concerns the way how rules facilitate the performance of illocutionary acts. Searle points out that rules associate illocutionary acts with certain effects *which are not natural effects*:

„For the case of promises and statements there must be some conventional elements the utterance of which counts as an undertaking of an obligation or the commitment to the existence of some state of affairs in order for it to be possible to perform such speech acts as promising or stating. The things specified in the rules are not natural effects, like feeling a pain, which one can cause apart from invoking any rules at all.“[57]

(c) This is related to the third consideration to be made concerning the assertion that language is a rule-regulated activity. This third consideration consists in a distinction between two kinds of rules: constitutive rules, and regulative rules.[58] The kind of rules relevant for language is that of constitutive rules. Searle understands the distinction as follows:

„[C]onstitutive rules do not merely regulate, they create or define new forms of behavior. [...] Regulative rules regulate a pre-existing activity, an activity whose existence is logically independent of the rules. Constitutive rules constitute (and also regulate) an activity the existence of which is logically dependent on the rules.“[59]

The common form of regulative rules is that of an imperative: 'Do *X*!', or 'If *Y*, then do *X*!'. The common form of constitutive rules is '*X* counts as *Y*' or '*X* counts as *Y* in context *C*'. Constitutive rules are not exclusively related to language; there are other types of actions – non-linguistic actions such as chess or football – which also depend on that

[56] Ibid. pp. 39 f.; emphasis added.

[57] Ibid. p. 40.

[58] That same distinction can be found in other writers, such as von Wright, Alf Ross, etc. It has been extensively discussed in recent legal philosophy. For a comparison of Searle's constitutive rules and von Wright's defining rules as well as for some problems with this distinction, cf., e. g., González Lagier 1993, p. 269.

[59] Searle 1969, pp. 33 f.

kind of rules.[60] Depending on whether or not actions or facts depend on such rules, we speak of institutional or of natural actions or facts.[61]

The constitutive nature of those rules is related to another peculiarity they are said to have, namely, their „almost tautological" condition:

„If our paradigms of rules are imperative regulative rules, such non-imperative constitutive rules are likely to strike us as extremely curious and hardly even as rules at all. Notice that they are almost tautological in character, for what the 'rule' seems to offer is part of a definition of 'checkmate' or 'touchdown'. That, for example, a checkmate in chess is achieved in such and such a way can appear now as a rule, now as an analytic truth based on the meaning of 'checkmate in chess'. That such statements can be construed as analytic is a clue to the fact that the rule in question is a constitutive one."[62]

The analytic character of these rules, in turn, is related to the question of their efficacy. According to Searle, not all constitutive rules come equipped with sanctions („after all, what penalty is there for violating the rule that baseball is played with nine men on a side?"[63]); and, what's more, „Indeed, it is not easy to see how one could even violate the rule as to what constitutes checkmate in chess, or touchdown in football".[64] Any deviation from the rules of a game does not imply a violation of those rules, but an 'exit' from the game, the playing of a different game. In that sense, then, that efficacy of constitutive rules is „necessary".

5.2.2. „We learned how to play the game of illocutionary acts, but in general it was done without an explicit formulation of the rules".[65] In order to determine what those rules are, Searle suggests that we search for the conditions that are necessary for the successful performance of a particular illocutionary act.

After analyzing different illocutionary acts, he lists the following kinds of conditions:

(a) Preparatory conditions: They „concern the right of the performer to carry out the act, the authority with which he must have been invested for it, as well as the conditions that must be satisfied on a particular speech-occasion to make its performance

[60] The assertion that constitutive rules create new ways of conduct can be comprehended better if one remembers the distinction between bodily movements and interpretations of bodily movements. What constitutive rules 'create' is the possibility of new interpretations of bodily movements. „It is possible that twenty-two men might go through the same physical movements as are gone through by two teams at a football game, but if there were no rules of football, that is, no antecedently existing game of football, there is no sense in which their behavior could be described as playing football" (Searle 1969, pp. 35 f.).

[61] Ibid. ch. 2.7.

[62] Ibid. p. 34.

[63] Ibid. p. 41.

[64] Ibid. p. 42.

[65] Ibid. p. 55.

possible".[66] If one or more of these prerequisites are violated, the respective speech act cannot be performed.

(b) Sincerity conditions: They refer to the appropriate beliefs or emotions the speaker must have in performing the act. If they are violated, this does not necessarily mean that the speech act is not performed, but it implies a verbal 'abuse'.

(c) The condition of propositional content: This concerns the minimal descriptive content any speech act has (for example, in the case of a promise, a future action of the speaker is described, etc.).

(d) Essential conditions: They refer to the kind of commitments the speaker incurs through the fact of having said such-and-such words.

Table 5. 1, on the next page, offers a comparison of the conditions of several illocutionary acts.

To these specific conditions, some general conditions must be added, e. g., that the normal *input* and *output* conditions obtain („that the speaker and the hearer both know how to speak the language", that there are „no physical impediments to communication", etc.) and that the speaker intends to produce in the hearer knowledge of what the essential condition of his utterance is, where the recognition of that intention is based, in turn, on his knowledge of the meaning of the utterance. That last condition captures the intuitions of Grice and amends them regarding the type of intention (the effect that must be produced is not a belief, an intention, etc., but the mere recognition of the essential condition for the illocutionary act) and the foundation of that recognition (it must be based on the knowledge of the conventional meaning of the utterance).[67]

Once these conditions have been determined, they can be formulated as rules that must be complied if an illocutionary act is to be successfully performed.

5.3. ‚A TAXONOMY OF ILLOCUTIONARY ACTS'

We have seen that Austin has offered a rough classification of illocutionary forces; but his proposal is plagued by several defects which Searle has summarized as follows: „there is a persistent confusion between verbs and acts, not all the verbs are illocutionary

Table 5.1

	Stating, asserting	**Ordering**	**Promising**
Preparatory conditions	(1) *S* has evidence (reasons to believe in the truth) of *p* (2) Neither for *S* nor for *L* is it obvious that *L* knows that *p*	(1) *L* is able to do *A* (2) Neither for *S* nor for *L* is it obvious that *L* will do *A* spontaneously in the normal course of	(1) *L* prefers that *S* does *A* rather than that he doesn't (2) *S* believes that *L* prefers that he does *A* rather than that he

[66] Acero/Bustos/Quesada 1982, p. 214.

[67] Searle 1969, pp. 57 ff.

		events (3) *S* has authority over *L*	doesn't (3) Neither for *S* nor for *L* is it obvious that *S* will do *A* in the normal course of events
Sincerity condition	*S* believes that *p*	*S* wants *L* to do *A*	*S* intends to do *A*
Condition of propositional content	any proposition *p*	*L*'s future act *A*	*S*'s future act *A*
Essential condition	counts primarily as acknowledgement that *p* represents a real state of affairs	counts primarily as an attempt by *S* to make *L* do *A*, by his authority	*S* intends his utterance to put him under the obligation of doing *A*

S = speaker, *L* = hearer, *A* = action

verbs, there is too much overlap of the categories, there is too much heterogeneity within the categories, many of the verbs listed in the categories don't satisfy the definition given for the category and, most important, there is no consistent principle of classification".[68] With the new concepts introduced in his own speech-act theory, Searle himself, in his paper 'A Taxonomy of Illocutionary Acts', offers a classification that he thinks overcomes these problems.

Searle presents twelve criteria on which to group different kinds of illocutionary acts into classes. Of these criteria, he mentions three as having special relevance: the point or purpose of an illocutionary act, the direction of fit between words and the world, and sincerity conditions.[69] Let us now look at these criteria somewhat more closely.

[68] Searle 1979a, pp. 11 f.

[69] The other criteria are: differences in the force or intensity with which the illocutionary object is presented; differences in the status or position of speaker and hearer insofar as that affects the illocutionary force of the utterance; differences in the way how the utterance is related to the speaker's and the hearer's interests; differences in how it is related to the rest of the discourse; differences in propositional content that are determined by the determinants indicating the illocutionary force; differences between acts that must always be speech acts and acts that may, but need not be performed as speech acts; differences between acts that require extra-linguistic institutions for their performance and those that do not; differences between acts where the

The point or purpose of an illocutionary act (Searle sometimes calls this the illocutionary point) corresponds to the most important of the conditions we have seen in the previous section, i. e., the essential condition. As Hierro remarks, it must be noted that Searle is not referring to the intention or purpose *of the speaker*, but to the purpose *of the act*.[70] In this way, Searle wants to exclude any possible intention to perform a perlocutionary act. What is relevant for the classification of illocutionary acts is not any intention the speaker might have and wish to realize through language, but only the intention conventionally linked to the performance of a particular illocutionary act (thus, orders express the intention to make the hearer do something, descriptions the intention to express a belief, promises the intention to incur an obligation on the part of the speaker, etc.).

The second notion relevant for the classification of illocutionary acts is that of 'direction of fit':

„Some illocutions have as part of their illocutionary point to get the words (more strictly, their propositional content) to match the world, others to get the world to match the words. Assertions are in the former category, promises and requests are in the latter.“[71]

Searle explains the concept of direction of fit with an example taken from Elizabeth Anscombe: „Suppose a man goes to the supermarket with a shoppinglist given him by his wife on which are written the words 'beans, butter, bacon, and bread'. Suppose as he goes around with his shopping cart selecting these items, he is followed by a detective who writes down everything he takes. As they emerge from the store, both shopper and detective will have identical lists. But the function of the two lists will be quite different. In the case of the shopper's list the purpose of the list is, so to speak, to get the world to match the words“ (world-to-words direction of fit). If when the buyer gets home his wife points out to him that he has bought pork chops instead of bacon, the mistake cannot be corrected by changing the list. The purpose of the detective's list, in contrast, is „to make the words match the world“ (words-to-world direction of fit), which means that „If the detective gets home and suddenly realizes that the man bought pork chops instead of bacon“, he can indeed correct the mistake simply by changing the list.[72]

Finally, the sincerity condition – which we have already seen a few lines above – refers to the speaker's mental state (belief, desire, feeling of satisfaction or sadness about something, etc.).

With these three criteria in mind, Searle's classification of illocutionary acts can now be presented in the following table:

corresponding illocutionary verb has a performative use and those where this is not the case; and differences in the style in which the illocutionary act is performed; cf. Searle 1979a, pp. 12 ff.

70 Hierro. S. Pescador 1982, p. 164.

71 Searle 1979a, p. 3.

72 Ibid. pp. 3 f.; cf. Anscombe 1963, p. 56.

Table 5.2

Type of act	Purpose	Direction of fit	Mental state
Assertive (describing, asserting, uttering, declaring)	to commit *S* to the belief that something is the case	words-to-world	belief
Directive (ordering, asking requesting, begging)	to get *L* to do *A*	world-to-words	desire that *L* do *A*
Commissive (promising)	to commit *S* to do *A*	world-to-words	intention of doing *A*
Expressive (thanking, excusing, congratulating)	to express *S*'s mental state	---	(depends on the mental state to be expressed)
Declarative (naming, resigning, firing, baptizing)	to bring about a change in some situation	world-to-words and words-to-world	(irrelevant)

This table requires three explanations. First, according to Searle, expressive acts have no direction of fit because they are neither an attempt to make the words fit the world nor an attempt to make the world fit the words; thus, if we ask to be forgiven for accidentally having stepped on another's foot, our purpose is neither to inform the other of that fact nor to invite anyone else to do likewise.[73] Second, Searle says that declarations have a double direction of fit, but his explanation of why that is so is obscure:

[73] Searle 1979a, pp. 15 f.

„The reason [...] is that declarations do attempt to get language to match the world. But they do not attempt to do it either by describing an existing state of affairs (as do assertives) nor by trying to get someone to bring about a future state of affairs (as do directives and commissives).“[74]

Third, according to Searle, the mental state is irrelevant for declarations. He thereby seems to suggest that the effect is produced independently of the speaker's mental state. An exception from this, he says, are what he calls 'assertive declarations', which are somewhere between declarations and assertions, such as acts of declaring someone guilty or of signaling a foul in soccer. Such acts have an assertive dimension insofar as they involve ascertaining and reflecting on reality (and they must satisfy the sincerity condition: a judge must believe that the accused is guilty, and a referee that there really was a foul), but they also have declarative force: once an accused has been declared guilty by a judge, he *is* guilty in legal terms.[75]

5.4. INTENTION AND ILLOCUTIONARY ACTS

Although Searle ascribes an important role to rules and conventions, the speaker's intention is no less relevant for him (his later explications of 'meaning' even focus on the notion of intention and intentionality in general and are linked to a theory of mind).[76] In Searle's theory, the relationship between intention and illocutionary act is manifest in at least two points:

(a) Intention$_1$: First of all, one of the conditions common to the performance of all speech acts is, as we have seen, that the speaker must have the intention that the hearer recognize the essential condition of the speech act to be performed (expressing a belief, attempting to get the hearer to do something, committing oneself to the performance of some future action, etc.). Intention$_1$ is common to all illocutionary acts. Searle calls it the 'communication intention'.[77]

(b) Intention$_2$: The second point of contact between illocutionary acts and intentions comes into play when we try to classify illocutionary acts. As we have seen, one of the criteria (which Searle regards as essential) is the illocutionary purpose or object of the act. That purpose is the intention the speaker expresses in performing one illocutionary act rather than another and which is conventionally linked to that illocutionary

[74] Ibid. p. 19.

[75] Ibid. pp. 16 ff.

[76] Searle performs this turn towards the theory of mind in his book *Intentionality* (1983).

[77] Searle 1983, pp. 165 f. In works published after *Speech Acts* (1969), Searle proposes to replace that 'communication intention' by a 'representation intention' as the key notion for understanding the meaning of an utterance. That 'representation intention' is prior to the communication intention and consists of the speaker's intention to make his utterance express or represent a certain mental state (belief, desire, etc.) and certain conditions that are necessary for the success of the illocutionary act. Thus, a description represents a belief and a situation of the world with which the utterance stands in a words-to-world direction of fit; an order represents a desire and a situation of the world with which the utterance stands in a world-to-words direction of fit, etc. (ibid., pp. 163 ff.). With this strategy, Searle wants to explain how it is possible that we sometimes make fully meaningful utterances without worrying about the reactions of the audience (nor about whether there is an audience at all), as when we simply 'think aloud'.

act. Intention$_2$ corresponds to the essential condition of each illocutionary act. Thus, if it is the essential condition of descriptions that they are expressions of beliefs, the corresponding intention$_2$ is the intention that the utterance count as the expression of a belief (whether that belief really exists is a question concerning the sincerity condition and is not relevant for the success of the illocutionary act).

What has just been explained permits us to say that there is a conceptual relationship between illocutionary acts and intention.[78] In contrast, perlocutionary acts do not have this relationship with intentions; they may, but need not be intentional. Whether or not there is an intention of performing a perlocutionary act serves, at best, to distinguish, as Austin does, between a *perlocutionary object* and a *perlocutionary sequel*.[79]

6. Conclusions

Linguistic pragmatics has contributed some solutions that can be extended to the theory of action. Here, I will mention only a few of them:

(1) the distinction between locutionary, illocutionary, and perlocutionary acts, which may perhaps be extended – with some modifications – to non-intentional actions;

(2) Grice's distinction between occasional, timeless, and applied timeless meaning (which may serve to qualify and complement the distinction between generic and individual actions, although I will not pursue this point in the present investigation);

(3) the distinction between natural and institutional actions and the corresponding distinction between regulative and constitutive rules; and

(4) the interrelation between intentions and conventions that can be found in some actions (e. g., in illocutionary actions and certain kinds of institutional actions).

Besides, some of the debates within linguistic pragmatics also show the tension between the intentional and the social point of view concerning actions.

[78] This is clearer in Searle's theory than in Austin's who seems to suggest the possibility of non-intentional illocutionary acts. Cf. Austin 1976, p. 106.

[79] Cf. above, sect. 4.2.

CHAPTER VI

THE PARADOXES DISSOLVED

1. Recapitulation. The Aspects of Action

1.1. NATURALISTIC, SUBJECTIVIST, AND SOCIAL THEORIES OF ACTION

A quick review of the theories of action we have seen in Chapters III and IV, advocated by philosophers and by criminal lawyers, respectively, will reveal parallels between them. Here, instead of explaining more about them in so many words, I will simply present them in the following table (where in the right-hand column, corresponding to criminal law, I will additionally indicate in brackets the equivalent approaches in Anglo-Saxon law):

Table 6.1

Philosophy of Action	Criminal Law
(1) Minimizing theories	(1) Causal theory of action (orthodox theory)
(2) G. H. von Wright (action as an intentional concept	(2) Teleological theory of action (subjectivism)
(3) H. L. A. Hart (action as a social concept	(3) Social theory of action (objectivism

The theories on the first level can be called 'naturalistic', those on the second level 'subjectivist', and those on the third level 'objectivist' or 'social' theories. Each group of theories refers to another dimension of actions: to the natural, the individual, and the social dimension, respectively. The differences between the theories of action we have seen in the preceding chapters can be understood as the result of emphasizing only one of these dimensions and neglecting the others. But such partial views face certain problems:

Naturalistic theories, for instance, show how actions are rooted in the real world; but, on the one hand, they shift the distinction between intentional and non-intentional actions from the realm of reality to that of language[1] and, on the other, they cannot account for the fact that actions are a subject of valorations and the content of norms.[2] Normative systems rarely refer merely to bodily movements; for the evaluation of an action, the circumstances and consequences following from bodily movements must be taken into account too. One way of solving this problem is to say that what norms contain is not classes of actions, but generic descriptions of actions (understood as voluntary bodily movements) in the light of the circumstances in which they are performed and of their possible consequences. But that seems rather awkward. In my view, the concept of action underlying our legal systems – as well as our morality – is not a concept that identifies action merely with voluntary bodily movements, but one that identifies action with voluntary bodily movements *interpreted* in the light of its circumstances and effects.

Subjectivist theories, in turn, are more adequate for explaining the possibility of the evaluation of actions, since they offer a criterion of interpretation, namely, intention. But by adopting exclusively the agent's point of view, they can account only for intentional actions. Sometimes, however, from our observers' perspective we evaluate the unintended consequences of actions and we say that they are things the agents have done; that is, we speak of non-intentional actions or, at least, actions that go beyond an agent's intention. And these are actions subjectivist theories cannot properly account for.[3]

Social theories, finally, can be understood in a weak or in a strong sense. In the weak sense, they emphasize the relevance of social rules and standards for the interpretation or meaning of actions. There is nothing to object against this weak version. Let me observe only that language offers us a large spectrum of names for classes of actions by which we can classify bodily movements (though it is wrong to think that there is an action verb for every possible action), and that many actions depend on the existence of systems of rules which constitute them in the first place (institutional actions). In the strong version, the social theory claims that the only valid criteria for the interpretation of actions, including intentional actions, are the criteria constituted by social rules. That version thus distorts the idea of intention which, instead of a subjective mental state, is now understood as an objective interpretation of an action.[4] When taken to the extreme, this objective concept of intention, depending on social criteria, implies the confusion of intention itself with the criteria and principles observers use in order to discover the intention of agents.

1.2. THE COMPLEMENTARINESS OF THE THREE GROUPS OF THEORIES. BASIC ACT, RESULT-ACT AND CONSEQUENCE-ACT. ACT AND ACTION

[1] Cf. sect. 1.1.2 of Chapter III.

[2] Cf. sects. 2.1 and 3.1 of Chapter IV.

[3] Cf. sect. 2 of Chapter III and sect. 2.2 of Chapter IV.

[4] Cf. sect. 3 of Chapter III and sect. 2.4 of Chapter IV.

In my view, we will be able to overcome these problems and the paradoxes of action only if we accept the 'three-dimensional' nature of action. Hence, a complete account of action can be given only if each one of these dimensions and of the corresponding positions is given due attention. Whenever we act, we can distinguish *(1)* certain voluntary bodily movements, *(2)* what we intentionally do by way of these bodily movements, and *(3)* the socially relevant consequences of *(2)*. In studying each one of these three elements, we probably may not disregard any of the three dimensions (the natural, the subjective, and the social). But, on the other hand, there can also be no doubt that whichever point of view we adopt will bring out the respective aspect of action with particular clarity. Thus, if we analyze actions from a naturalistic perspective, the aspect that will appear more strongly than the others is the first; if we approach actions from a subjective perspective, the outstanding aspect will be the second; and if we adopt a social perspective, the third aspect will become more strongly visible. What we must try to avoid is the reductionist temptation, i. e., to make any one of these aspects of action the exclusive and central object of attention, since each one of them accounts for some important characteristic of actions, without being able to explain others. The fact that the reductionist temptation has not always been successfully avoided has been responsible for what in the previous chapters I have called the profound ambiguity of the term 'action', because through a process of metonymy each aspect has given rise to a different sense of the word. Thus, *(1)*, *(2)*, and *(3)* are, at the same time, different aspects of action understood as a whole, and different meanings of the term 'action' as it is commonly used.

I have called *(1)* the basic act, *(2)* the result-act, and *(3)* the consequence-act. I think this terminology may be useful in accounting for certain controversies without the burdens of traditional terminology. Besides, it is related to notions that are widely used in the analytical philosophy of action, such as Arthur Danto's concept of basic action, or von Wright's distinction between result and consequence. Actually, the concepts this terminology refers to are the same as those we can refer to by using more common expressions, such as 'voluntary action', 'intentional action', and 'non-intentional action', provided we give a certain meaning to 'voluntariness' and 'intention'. However, the latter three expressions are highly ambiguous, and perhaps their meaning has been clarified somewhat by relating them to the notion of basic action, result and consequence.

My analysis of the concept of action seems to lead to an inevitable conclusion: If the 'basic act', the 'result-act' and the 'consequence-act' are, on the one hand, three different aspects of action understood as a whole and, on the other, each one of them is also considered an action by itself, we are facing a new ambiguity which we must try to dissolve. In order to do that, it may be useful to refer to each of these aspects as an 'act', and reserve the term 'action' for their conjunction as a whole.

1.3. THE ASPECTS OF ACTION AND THE DISTINCTION BETWEEN LOCUTIONARY, ILLOCUTIONARY AND PERLOCUTIONARY ACTS

The distinction, proposed by Austin for speech acts, between the locutionary, the illocutionary, and the perlocutionary aspect or act can be seen as a special case – applying to linguistic actions, and therefore requiring some modifications – of the three aspects of action in general. According to a general theory of action along these lines, one and the same bodily movement could be described as a mere bodily movement (basic act), or with a view towards the agent's intention to produce a certain change (result-act), or with a view towards consequences, beyond what is intended (consequence-act). According to speech-act theory, one and the same bodily movement – which normally consists in the production of certain sounds in certain circumstances – may be individuated or described in a generic and, if I may say so, rather uninterpreted way as an act of 'saying' something (locutionary act), or with a view towards the intention expressed by the agent, which is conventionally linked to certain words (illocutionary act), or with a view towards the effects or consequences of the utterance on the audience (perlocutionary act), regardless of whether or not they are intended.

But it would be premature to take the two distinctions to be simply equivalent. Due to the peculiarities of linguistic actions, there are indeed some differences between the three kinds or aspects of a speech act, and the notions of basic act, result-act and consequence-act. Perhaps one can say that Austin's distinction inspires the distinction between basic act, result-act and consequence-act, without being exactly the same, and perhaps not even, strictly speaking, a special case of the latter. Thus, a locutionary act is not merely an uninterpreted bodily movement; rather, it includes the utterance of certain words fitting certain conventions and with a meaning and a reference. But that can be explained by the fact that for a theory of speech acts aimed at accounting for the notion of the meaning of an utterance, the analysis of mere bodily movements is not particularly useful. The relevant basic unit of such a theory is 'saying' something (which, seen from a more general perspective, already includes an interpretation of the action). Strictly speaking, a parallel exists between a phonetic act and a basic act (that is, the phonetic act is a kind of basic act). Now, regarding the illocutionary act, the fact that the conventional aspect of language must be accounted for implies that not every linguistic act individuated by a result is an illocutionary act (in contrast to what is the case with result-acts). For an act to be an illocutionary act, it must be individuated by the result that is intended by the agent, and that result must be linked conventionally (through a constitutive rule) to the performance of such an act. But this only means that illocutionary acts are institutional actions which depend on rules or conventions (such a link between intentions and conventions also appears in certain kinds of institutional actions that are of special relevance in the law, more specifically, those performed by using a power-conferring rule[5]). Finally, perlocutionary acts may or may not be intentional, whereas, according to what I have said earlier, consequence-acts are not intentional. However, there are still parallels between the two, in the sense that the notion of a perlocutionary act, just like the notion of a consequence-act and in contrast to the notion of an illocutionary act, has no *conceptual* relation with intention.[6]

In any case, it must be underscored that Austin's distinction points into the same direction as the distinctions of philosophers and criminal lawyers, with the necessary adjustments for speech acts; but Austin has an advantage over them because he realized that these are three aspects of actions (or kinds of acts) that cannot be reduced to one.

[5] On power-conferring rules, cf. Atienza/Ruiz Manero 1998.

[6] Cf. sect. 5.4 of Chapter IV.

1.4. CRITERIA FOR THE DISTINCTION BETWEEN THE THREE ASPECTS OF ACTION

The peculiarities of these three aspects of action are given in the following table:

Table 6.2

Aspect of action	*Attribution of meaning*	*Element with highest weight in interpretation*	*Point of view adopted in the interpretation*	*Function of the sentences referring to each aspect*
Basic act	Basic meaning	---	---	Non-interpretive description
Result-act	Full meaning	Result (change intended)	Agent's point of view (intentional)	Interpretive description
Consequence-act	Full meaning	Consequence (changes beyond intention)	Others' point of view (social)	Ascription

On the basis of this table, the following observations can be made:

(1) One of the criteria which allow us to distinguish between the three aspects of actions is the 'meaning' or interpretation the actions can be given. For the time being, it is enough to stipulate that the 'meaning of an action' is that which makes us subsume that action under some class of actions.[7] Thus, the meaning of 'flexing one's finger' may be that of 'firing a gun', 'killing someone', or 'making a joke' (or simply 'flexing one's finger').

(2) Basic acts are an aspect of actions without meaning in the strict sense. In other words, when we concentrate on this aspect of an action, we are not interested in attributing a meaning to it. That does not mean that there is no interpretation at all in the case of basic acts. As we know, basic acts correspond to the naturalistic dimension of actions and therefore consist in sequences of bodily movements (although not every sequence of bodily movements is a basic act). Now, the description of a sequence of bodily movements as a basic act requires *(a)* the verification that the bodily movement arises from the agent's intention, i. e., that it is voluntary (a widely accepted criterion in order to distinguish between mere reflex movements and actions is whether or not the bodily movements were performed voluntarily, that is, with the intention or the desire to bring about some change, whatever that change may be), and *(b)* a use of language that already contains a minimum of interpretation (I cannot describe the bodily movement consisting in the bending of a finger without using the verb that corresponds to the action class of 'bending'). These two elements presuppose a certain degree of interpre-

[7] Cf. sect. 6 of Chapter VII.

tation of bodily movements, but that is minimal in comparison with the interpretation implied in the assertion of an action of killing, or of closing a door. While in the former case, what is asserted is that there is an action and what is described are mere bodily movements, in the latter case what is asserted is what kind of action – in other terms than those of mere bodily movements – it is. For such a minimal interpretation, it is enough to describe directly what we observe, without relating it to a context, an intention, or an effect. Hence, we can say that basic acts have a basic meaning, while result-acts and consequence-acts have full meaning.

(3) When we focus on the other two aspects of an action, we adopt an 'interpretive attitude', that is, we are interested in attributing a meaning to the basic act. That is why we can say that a result-act and a consequence-act have a full meaning. 'What has the agent done?', we ask. The answer is usually the result of subsuming the respective bodily movements under a generic class of actions other than that of the mere bodily movements. We can answer the question from the agent's point of view (giving a description that is interpreted with a view towards the agent's intended object, that is, the *result* of the action) or from a social point of view (the element which allows us to individuate the action in that case is a *consequence*, in von Wright's terminology). When we interpret the action from a social point of view, we do so because, in the light of some social rules and standards, there are certain circumstances which cause the action – in the words of Manuel Cruz – to „transcend the limits of the purely private. When this is the case, no matter how tolerant we are, our attention shifts from the protagonist to the effects of his conduct. Intentions lose importance, and are displaced by results“.[8]

(4) It is difficult to spell out precisely what circumstances make us ascribe to an agent some particular consequence-act from the chain of effects triggered by his bodily movements. Among the criteria we use are the following: the distance between the bodily movements and the considered effect, its foreseeability, its social relevance (which depends, in turn, on whether or not it is given consideration in some system of rules and on the relevance of that system), the presence or absence of interferences in the chain of causes and effects, and so on.[9]

(5) There is a certain parallel between the interpretation of texts and the interpretation of bodily movements (basic acts). To interpret a text is to correlate that text with a possible meaning; to interpret a bodily movement is to correlate that movement with a generic class of actions. And just as in order to determine the meaning of a text we can refer either to the intention of its author (subjective interpretation) or, on the contrary, to the social effects of our interpretation, in order to interpret a bodily movement an observer can refer to the agent's intention or to social criteria.

(6) If we take the comparison between the interpretation of texts and the interpretation of actions a step further, the following can be said: Just as when interpreting a text according to social criteria we presuppose that the author of the text had the intention to give that text a certain meaning – and that, therefore, there is a subjective meaning of the text, although it does not interest us at the moment –, when interpreting a bodily movement from a social or objective point of view we presuppose

[8] Cruz 1990, p. 110.

[9] Cf. Chapter VII, Sect. 6.3.

that the agent performed that movement with a particular intention – and that, therefore, that bodily movement does have a subjective meaning.

(7) Result-acts are an aspect of action the interpretation of which presupposes the agent's point of view; consequence-acts have a meaning that presupposes an observer's point of view. What characterizes these two aspects of action is not who does the interpreting of the bodily movement (nor whether anyone does in fact interpret it), but the point of view implied in the meaning. Thus, an agent may interpret his own action from the point of view of the socially relevant consequences it brings about (an example of this is Oedipus who, when he discovered that, though unintentionally, he had killed his father and married his mother, tore his eyes out); and an observer may interpret an action from the agent's point of view, in which case he will attempt to find out what the agent's intention was (that this is the adopted point of view becomes apparent when an observer manifests his willingness to change his interpretation if he can be convinced that the agent's intention was not what the observer thinks it was; if that willingness is lacking, then the adopted point of view is that of a third party).

(8) The last criterion for the distinction between the three aspects of action is the linguistic function of the sentences that refer to these aspects. Basic acts and result-acts appear in descriptive (pre-interpretive and interpretive, respectively) sentences. This implies that to say that Princip intentionally killed the Archduke (assuming a subjective sense of intention) is a matter of truth or falsity. In some cases, it may be difficult to determine whether or not there was an intention, but that does not mean that answers to the question are not true or false. In contrast, when we say that Princip brought about World War I (assuming that this was not his intention), we impute an action to him. In that case, it is not an appropriate way of speaking to say that it is true or false that Princip brought about World War I. Properly speaking, what is at issue is whether or not it is correct to ascribe such an action to Princip, according to the criteria mentioned above (the foreseeability of the event, the length of the causal chain, etc.). In other words, while result-acts are relative to the agent's intention, consequence-acts are relative to those social criteria.

Following Feinberg, I think that the ascriptive or attributive function of language (in a strong sense) differs in at least three aspects from the descriptive function: *(i)* it implies an irreducible degree of discretion (in the last instance, it is not a matter of *discovery*, but of *decision*); *(ii)* it is context-dependent (that is, our interest in attributing an action to this or that agent, or in attributing to an agent this or that action, is context-dependent); and *(iii)* it is 'defeasible' (i. e., such attributions are of a *prima facie* nature).[10] What I am trying to suggest is that our attitude toward intentional actions is primarily descriptive, and our attitude toward non-intentional actions is primarily ascriptive.

[10] Feinberg 1968, pp. 111 ff. As we have seen in Chapter III, Sect. 3, Feinberg adds that the ascription of an action is performed in order to attribute responsibility (in the widest sense, including merely causal responsibility which does not necessarily imply blame); but we do not need to include this feature here, because he stretches the meaning of 'responsibility' too far. For the present context, it is enough to say that when an action is ascribed to someone, this is normally done with some purpose (which must not necessarily be that of blaming or praising).

2. The Paradoxes of Action Reconsidered

These three aspects of actions give rise to what I have called in Chapter I the 'profound ambiguity' of action. As we have seen, the term 'action' can be interpreted as 'basic act', 'result-act', or 'consequence-act', or as the conjunction of all three aspects. The paradoxes we have seen in Chapter II can be regarded as the result of using the same term ('action') in different senses.

2.1. SOLUTION OF THE FIRST PARADOX

The first paradox concerns the question whether actions (not the concept of action, but every particular action) are natural phenomena or a conceptual construction resulting from our view of the world. If by 'action' one understands 'basic act', the answer is: actions are the former (natural phenomena) rather than the latter (conceptual constructions), although, no doubt, the two are not entirely separated. If by 'action' one understands 'result-act' or 'consequence-act', then, since we adopt an 'interpretive attitude' toward those aspects, the answer is: the latter rather than the former. Besides, that nature of a conceptual construction is more pronounced in the case of consequence-acts – where the criteria of interpretation are independent of intention – than in the case of result-acts. Intention is a human mental state and, therefore, a natural phenomenon, but at the same time it is a phenomenon the content of which is intrinsically linked to the 'conceptual world'. Hence, intention can be seen as a 'bridge' between the natural and the interpretive dimension of actions.

2.2. SOLUTION OF THE SECOND PARADOX

According to the second paradox, there is a tension between the consideration of actions as mere bodily movements, or as descriptions or interpretations of such movements. That paradox can be solved as follows: It is true that actions consist in bodily movements if by 'action' we understand 'basic act'. And it is also true that one and the same bodily movement can give rise to different actions in different circumstances, and that one and the same class of actions can be performed through different bodily movements, if by 'action' we understand the interpretation of a bodily movement.

2.3. SOLUTION OF THE THIRD PARADOX

The third paradox concerned the question whether there is some privileged point of view for the interpretation of actions. When we say that an agent cannot be wrong about his own actions,[11] 'action' must be understood in the sense of 'result-act'. An observer may try to find out what the intention of the agent is and describe his action from the agent's point of view. In that case, the observer may err, and the agent has the last word (although that does not exclude that he may lie). When consequence-acts are imputed to

[11] In the sense spelled out in Chapter I, sect. 4.

someone, the content of the agent's intention does not matter (although some intention must have existed). In that case, the person doing the imputation may err, but the error does not consist in giving an inadequate description of the action, but in using the criteria which guide the imputation in an incorrect way.

2.4. SOLUTION OF THE FOURTH PARADOX

How many actions do we perform with one bodily movement? The answer must distinguish between basic act, result-act and consequence-act. If by 'action' we understand 'basic act', then with one sequence of bodily movements we perform a single action. If 'action' is taken to mean 'result-act', the answer is that we perform as many actions as there are changes we desire to bring about. Normally, such actions stand in a means-end relationship. If 'action' means 'consequence-act', the answer will depend on how many actions observers ascribe to the agent, in accordance with the criteria for the ascription of actions. Not every consequence of our bodily movements constitutes an action – only those which are interpreted as such, according to those criteria.

But there is another sense in which we can understand the question: Whenever we do something, how many aspects of an action are involved? The answer is that when someone acts, what can be distinguished is always a basic act which (unless it is merely a reflex-act) is necessarily accompanied at least by a result-act; in addition, consequence-acts may perhaps be imputed.

Here, we can recall Nino's example which was mentioned earlier, in Section 5 of Chapter II. Nino asked how many actions are performed by beggars who mutilate children in order to provoke more compassion, when some of the children die as a consequence of the mutilations. In my view, the answer must be that in each case the beggars perform one single basic act (the bodily movements which bring about the mutilation), one result-act (the mutilation), and one consequence-act (the causation of death). Perhaps some more result-acts can be distinguished, namely, those which are means for the mutilation; but they are then just so many phases of the action of mutilating. And perhaps also some other consequence of the mutilation may be imputed as an action.

2.5. SOLUTION OF THE FIFTH PARADOX

The fifth paradox involved the limits of our actions. The answer to the corresponding question depends, again, on the sense of action one adopts.

(1) If 'action' is understood as 'basic act', the answer is far from obvious. Where are the limits of the sequence of bodily movements constituting a basic act? Given a sequence of bodily movements, how do we know whether we are dealing with only one or with several basic acts? What we are looking for is some element in an action, understood simply as bodily movement, which can help us to solve the problem of the individuation of actions. The criterion we are looking for may not refer to the interpretation of bodily movements, because then we would not be individuating a basic act directly, as such, but only indirectly, through a result-act or a consequence-act.

The major 'candidate' for a criterion of that kind is the continuity or discontinuity of bodily movements. Actions seem to have temporal limits. This is evidenced by the fact that when an agent's conduct stretches over time, rather than an 'action' we usually call it an 'activity'. For instance, 'pursuing a course of studies', 'writing a novel', 'building a house' all seem to be sequences of actions, not a single global action. But if we take a closer look at that criterion of the continuity or discontinuity of the sequence of bodily movements, we come to realize that, as Nino observes, it is not a criterion which depends on the concept of action, but on the concepts of the respective particular actions ('to kill', 'to write a novel', etc.); i. e., it depends on the features which define a particular class of actions. Nino gives the following example: if someone kills another by lacing his food with poison every day for some number of days, we don't have several actions of killing, although we have several actions of poisoning. According to Nino, this is so because the action class of 'poisoning', by definition, requires temporal continuity, whereas the action class of 'killing' does not. But, obviously, in order to individuate a basic act through the application of that criterion, we must first interpret the bodily movements, that is, we must correlate the sequence of bodily movements with a class of actions; only then can we decide – depending on the connotation of the respective class of actions – how many basic acts we have.

The same applies to other possible criteria of individuation at the level of bodily movements. Nino suggests that we sometimes look at the 'form' of the movements: „when the cycle of characteristic movements is completed just once, even if in a discontinuous way, we say that there is one single action; and if that cycle, that *form*, is repeated, even in a temporally uninterrupted way, we generally say that there are several actions".[12] Again, the criterion depends on the class of actions which serves as reference and, therefore, is not independent of interpretation.

I think that this result can be generalized, and that one can say that the limits of a 'basic act' cannot be determined without prior interpretation of the bodily movements. But that there are no criteria for the individuation of basic acts which are not mediated through an interpretation of those acts is not a feature that is exclusive to them, or even to actions in general. The question about the individuation of actions raises problems that are very similar to those raised by the question for the individuation of events, or even of material objects; and in all these cases we take recourse to classes. As Donald Davidson (for whom actions are a kind of events[13]) observed:

> „Individuation at its best requires sorts or kinds that give a principle for counting. But here again, events come out well enough: rings of the bells, major wars, eclipses of the moon, and performances of *Lulu* can be counted as easily as pencils, pots, and people. Problems can arise in either domain. The conclusion to be drawn, I think, is that the individuation of events poses no problems worse in principle than the problems posed by individuation of material objects."[14]

Since there is no *direct* criterion for the individuation of basic acts, we must see whether there is an *indirect* criterion (that is, a criterion which refers to the

[12] Nino 1972, p. 37.

[13] Davidson 1980b, p. 113.

[14] Davidson 1980c, p. 180.

interpretation of bodily movements) that may be generalized (and of which the peculiarities of every particular concept of action are merely marginal adjustments).

We have seen that our problem translates into the question about the individuation of classes. And with respect to the individuation of classes of actions, the following question arises: Is it merely a linguistic matter which classes of actions we admit? Must there be a corresponding action verb for a class of actions to exist?

The classes of actions we are willing to admit cannot depend on language, since if that were the case the actions an agent can perform would vary not only as a function of his capacities and opportunities, but also as a function of the language spoken by him or the respective community. But there is another way for individuating classes of actions. It seems that we can say that classes of actions are defined on the grounds of changes. Hence, we could say that there are at least as many classes of actions as there are classes of changes ('at least', because two or more different actions might be defined for one and the same change) we can bring about through our bodily movements (including merely a movement of the body). Every class of actions is thus defined on the basis of a change, which may be the result or a consequence of the action (depending on whether we are speaking of a result-act or a consequence-act). This conception takes into account von Wright's idea that there is a conceptual connection between an action and a change in the world, but it does not reduce that connection to the relationship between an action and a result (understood as the change intended by the agent). I will call those changes which stand in a conceptual relationship with an action 'action-internal changes'.

Once the correlation between a bodily movement and a change in the world which constitutes such an 'internal change' has been established, we can indicate a criterion for the individuation of basic acts: Given a sequence of bodily movements, a single basic act is constituted by those, and only those, bodily movements which are *sufficient* to bring about the 'action-internal change'. This criterion requires two adjustments:

(a) Sometimes, bodily movements which contribute to the 'internal change' without being strictly necessary for bringing it about may also be considered part of the action (movements likely to assure that change).

(b) Some adjustments may be necessary because a class of actions has been incorporated into language that implies a modification of the general criterion with additional requirements (such as, for example, a certain characteristic 'form' of the action).

(2) Let us now look at the question of the limits of actions when 'action' is understood as 'result-act'. Here, we can use the following schematic representation:

$$I \text{ ------- } BM \text{ ------- } C_1 \text{ ------- } C_2 \text{ ------- } \ldots \text{ ------- } C_n$$

If we ask how far we can extend a result-act in the chain of changes induced by some bodily movements, the answer is that the action extends all the way to the change the agent intended to bring about (the result of the action). If the intention was, for instance, to bring about change C_2, then the result-act cannot be described by reference to any of the changes posterior to C_2. As we have seen, however, to the extent that the changes prior to C_2 are means for bringing about C_2, they also can give rise to the individuation of intentional actions, which are, however, different from the action of bringing about C_2, although they stand in a special relationship to it, similar to the relationship between a part and a whole.[15]

(3) Finally, if we ask about 'action' in the sense of 'consequence-action', that is, if we ask, using the same schematic representation, about the last change that can serve as a point of reference to describe the bodily movements, there is no single precise answer; rather, the answer depends on the relatively vague criteria mentioned before – which, besides, must be weighed against each other –, such as the length of the chain of consequences (the more remote they are from the bodily movement, the smaller their chance of being considered an 'action-internal change'), their relevance in the light of the system of rules used as a point of reference (the more relevant, the greater the chance), their foreseeability, etc.[16]

[15] Cf. González Lagier 1997.

[16] Cf. sect. 6.3 of Chapter VII.

CHAPTER VII

THE STRUCTURE OF ACTION

1. Introduction

In the previous chapter, I concluded that it may be useful for solving the paradoxes of action, or at least for taking a new look at some of the problems that have come up in philosophy and in criminal-law doctrine, to distinguish three aspects of actions (giving rise to three different meanings of the term 'action'). In this chapter, I will propose a framework that may be of use in the analysis of result-acts and consequence-acts. For that purpose, I will analyze *some* of the common elements we find *in a great number* of actions (if not in all of them) – for instance, in actions such as closing a window, killing another person, making a will, etc. – or, if you wish, in a great number of actions *under a particular description* (if one opts for a concept of action on the lines of Anscombe and Davidson).

We can distinguish (at least) the following 'elements' of actions:

(1) a sequence of bodily movements;
(2) an effect or change in the world;
(3) a connection between that sequence of bodily movements and that change in the world (or between one change and the other);
(4) an intention; and
(5) the interpretation or meaning of the sequence of bodily movements.

In the following sections, I will consider each one of them, in that order.

2. The Sequence of Bodily Movements

2.1. THE ROLE OF BODILY MOVEMENTS

Bodily movements are the element by which actions come into the world. On the one hand, from an observer's point of view, when he 'sees' an action what he actually sees is a sequence of bodily movements performed by an agent which are then interpreted in the light of that agent's intentions (more precisely, his assumed intentions) or of some rules. Bodily movements are, so to speak, the 'raw material' which we interpret. This guarantees that, rather than being purely conceptual entities, actions are rooted in the natural world, independently of whether they are natural or institutional actions. On the other hand, from the agent's own point of view, the performance of an action x_1 often consists in the performance of another action x_2 which stands in a special relationship with x_1 (I will call this a 'generational relation': x_2 generates – causally, conventionally, etc. – x_1). I air the room *by* opening the window, and I open the window *by* turning the knob. The first element of this process that is external to the agent ('external' in contrast with mental events) are the bodily movements: they 'release' the action into the external world.

On this view, actions must have an observable aspect. This excludes mental acts from the concept of action, but it does not exclude speech acts which, in the last instance, consist in the uttering of sounds for which bodily movements (of the throat, the mouth, the lips ...) are necessary. In this context, Habermas distinguishes causally relevant and semantically relevant bodily movements.[1] The latter category could be extended to account for all institutional actions. We could then speak of conventionally relevant bodily movements.

2.2. ANY BODILY MOVEMENT?

However, not *all* movements of our body are part of actions. When it comes to determining which bodily movements can be part of an action, there are various options. The answer depends partly on whether or not we are willing to include reflex-acts in our notion of action.

A first option is to say that only bodily movements that *can generically be controlled* by an agent can be elements of action. That excludes heartbeats, peristaltic bowel movements, spasms, etc., but it includes in the concept of action many so-called reflexes (which are different from heartbeats, peristaltic movements, etc.). This is so because the requirement that the bodily movements must be of a kind that the agent can *generically* control must not be confused with the requirement that they must be voluntary or intentional, nor with the requirement that in a particular case the agent must in fact have been able to control them. The controlability requirement is weaker. It only requires a class of bodily movements that *can* be performed intentionally. This is sufficient for saying that it is a class of movements an agent *can* control, regardless of whether or not in a particular case he may in fact have performed such movements intentionally. When I am stung by a mosquito and in a reflex slap it with my hand, I do not intentionally move my arm. But I *could* do the same thing intentionally. Hence, I do control that generic class of movements. We often perform bodily movements that are involuntary, but which on other occasions we can perform voluntarily. That is what reflex-acts are. And it may be convenient to have a concept of action that includes reflex-acts, because sometimes these can give rise to some kind of responsibility on the part of the agent. In that case, reflex-acts can be understood as basic acts (i. e., they can be described in terms of bodily movements) or as consequence-acts (i. e., they can be interpreted in the light of consequences and rules). But they cannot be understood as result-acts, which means that they cannot be given an intentional interpretation.

If we want to exclude reflex-acts from the realm of action, we must strengthen the controlability requirement and demand that the bodily movements must also be voluntary. But, as we will see later, the expression 'voluntariness' is extremely ambiguous. At this point, suffice it to say that the bodily movements which in that sense can form part of an action are those performed by an agent with some intention,

[1] Habermas 1988, vol. 1, p. 145.

regardless of what that intention is (thus, 'voluntariness' here means the fact that the movements are accompanied by some intention). It is that intention which actually 'controls' the movements of our body in a particular case. I will later come back to this requirement of intentionality.

2.3. LIMITS OF BODILY MOVEMENTS

Concerning the limits of the sequence of bodily movements that form part of an action, the problem is the same as in the case of basic acts. Hence, the considerations formulated in Section 2.4.1 of Chapter VI apply.

3. Changes in the World

3.1. DO ALL ACTIONS BRING ABOUT A CHANGE IN THE WORLD?

In order to answer the question whether all actions bring about a change in the world, we must first clarify some conceptual details. There is a weak sense in which it is trivial that all actions produce a change in the world: if action requires a movement of our body, and our bodies are part of the world, there is necessarily a change in the world whenever we perform an action. But often we cannot describe the change brought about by an action independently of the description of the bodily movements involved in that action. That is the case, for instance, when we ask about the change produced by actions such as 'bending a finger' or 'running': the answer usually is that the respective changes are precisely those of 'having bent a finger' or 'having run'. These are references to changes in a weak sense. But our bodily movements can also bring about other kinds of changes. They can bring it about, for example, that a door is closed, a jar breaks, a person dies, a forest burns, a war breaks out.

Hence, in a weak sense, all actions bring about an effect on, or a change in, the world; but in that weak sense the requirement of such an effect on the world simply coincides with the requirement of a bodily movement. In a strong sense, in contrast, many actions obviously do bring about some further change in the world, but not necessarily all actions bring about a sufficiently *relevant* change, beyond the bodily movements, to allow us to individuate the action with reference to that change.

3.2. 'ACTION-INTERNAL' CHANGE

In the light of what has just been observed, we can say that all actions are *conceptually* linked to a change (in the strong or, at least, in the weak sense) in the world.[2] I will call this kind of change an 'action-internal' change. In a way, this notion is an offspring of von Wright's notion of the 'result' of an action, but in contrast to the latter, it is independent of the agent's intention, thus allowing us to account for unintended as well as for intended actions. Both are defined in reference to some change, which we choose

[2] The link is conceptual because the action is defined by that change.

from the chain of changes a bodily movement may give rise to either because it is the change intended by the agent (intentional action) or in accordance with certain social principles or conventions (unintentional action).

3.3. NATURAL CHANGES AND INSTITUTIONAL CHANGES

A theory of action that is to be of use for legal considerations should distinguish between natural changes and institutional changes or effects, which are produced, so to speak, in two different 'worlds' – the 'natural world' and the 'normative world'. Natural changes are changes brought about independently of the existence of rules. Institutional changes or effects depend for their production on the existence of rules. This last assertion, however, must not be interpreted in a metaphysical sense. That a norm gives rise to a change or an action is to be understood merely in the sense that norms offer us a new framework for the interpretation of a natural change or the corresponding natural action.[3] A person's death is a natural change since it is entirely independent of rules. Rules may, of course, prohibit to bring about such a change; but the change itself can obviously be brought about independently of them. However, killing a person under certain circumstances constitutes (can be interpreted as) a homicide or murder. Committing homicide or murder is an institutional change, just like getting married or issuing a law. Once an institutional change has been brought about, it triggers a series of normative consequences (consisting, in the last instance, in the emergence of new rules, rights or duties), and that is why such changes can be described in the light of those consequences.[4]

3.4. FROM ONE WORLD TO THE OTHER

Bodily movements trigger a sequence of changes or effects, and the individuation of an action depends on which of the changes in the chain

$$I \text{ — } BM \text{ — } C_1 \text{ — } C_2 \text{ — } C_3 \text{ — } \ldots \text{ — } C_n$$

is taken to be relevant.

Now, the different changes in such a sequence may belong to different 'worlds'. By bending a finger, we may be pulling a trigger (i. e., bring about a natural change), thereby causing the death of a person (natural change) which, in turn, brings about certain normative consequences (institutional effects). By writing our name on a piece of paper (natural change), we may incur certain obligations (institutional effect). Institutional changes necessarily require a previous natural change; hence, in the last instance, institutional actions too depend on bodily movements.

3.5. ANY CHANGE?

[3] Cf. Searle 1969, pp. 50 ff.

[4] On the idea of institutional changes or results and their relationship to a certain kind of norms, cf. Atienza/ Ruiz Manero 1998, ch. II.3; also, Redondo 1999, ch. I.4.

Not all natural changes happening in the world can be part of an action: only those changes which we can basically bring about by bodily movements. But the expression 'can bring about' is too vague, even if understood in the factual (and not in the normative) sense. Thus, it is perhaps convenient to add a few observations, aiming at greater precision.

The distinction between what we can and what we cannot do is too sharp. Instead, I propose to distinguish between changes which (in some reasonable way) are within an agent's control (such as closing a door), changes which are beyond an agent's control (such as bringing about that it rains tomorrow), and changes which are partially within and partially beyond an agent's control (such as increasing the standard of living, or throwing a twelve at dice).[5] A change is within an agent's control when he can perform an action that is a reasonably sufficient condition for that change.[6] A change is entirely beyond an agent's control when he can perform no action which would be either such a sufficient condition or at least a condition that, though not sufficient, would contribute to the change. And, finally, a change is partially within an agent's control when he can perform actions which contribute to, but are not sufficient conditions for that change.

Obviously, changes which are reasonably within an agent's control can be part of actions, whereas changes which are entirely beyond an agent's control cannot. But the interesting question is, of course, what happens with the changes that are partially within an agent's control. Is it an action to bring about such a change? Or is it, in the last instance, only a consequence of bodily movements that does not belong to the universe of what we call 'action'? Is there such an action as 'increasing the standard of living' or 'throwing a twelve at dice'? The answer is far from obvious, and all we can say with certainty is that we are here moving in the zone of penumbra of the concept of action, because the conclusion we will draw in each particular case will depend on such circumstances as speech habits, or a greater or lesser influence of chance. Perhaps it may be suggested that these are things we do *with* our actions, instead of being directly actions of ours. To illustrate this with an example presented by John Searle:

„For example, if I intend to weigh 160 pounds by Christmas and I succeed, it won't do to say I performed the intentional action of weighing 160 pounds by Christmas nor will it do to say that weighing 160 pounds by Christmas can be an intentional action. What one wants to say rather is that if I fulfilled my intention to weigh

[5] Besides, the expression 'within/beyond an agent's control' may be understood to refer either to any agent in normal conditions, or to some particular agent.

[6] For the theory of action, the logical notion of a sufficient condition is too strong because we can never be sure that a bodily movement will actually be sufficient to bring about a certain change (other than that of the bodily movement itself). There are at least two reasons for this: first, the inductive nature of our knowledge about causal relations; and second, the fact that we can never be absolutely sure that the causal context at a particular moment in time is exactly the right one for bringing about an intended change, because we are incapable of analyzing all the relevant variables. That is why it seems convenient to speak of conditions which (in the light of what we know and what be believe to be able to do) are *reasonably* sufficient. Cf. on this González Lagier 1997.

160 pounds by Christmas, I must have performed certain *actions by means of which* I came to weigh 160 pounds [...]"[7]

As for institutional changes, what changes of that kind we can bring about depends on the respective system of norms. Basically, there seem to be no restrictions to the normative changes a system of norms may give rise to. But, in any case, the same restrictions we have already seen in the context of natural actions apply here too (i. e., that the change must be within, or at least partly within, the agent's control). After all, it must not be forgotten that an institutional change is nothing but an interpretation of a natural change.

4. The Link Between a Bodily Movement and a Change in the World

Since bodily movements bring about (natural or institutional) changes in the world, there must be some relationship, some link, between such movements and such changes. That link is of a causal nature in the case of natural changes, and of a conventional nature in the case of institutional changes.

4.1. CAUSAL RELATIONS

We usually understand the relation of causality as a kind of relationship that can be found in nature: if we heat a piece of metal, it will expand. The expansion of metals through heat is produced with a kind of necessity we can call 'natural necessity'[8] – the relation of causality is something like a physical necessity. It would go too far at this point to undertake a detailed analysis of cause-effect relationships, but it should at least be recalled that this way of presenting the topic, though not wrong, obscures the conventional and contextual nature of causality. As Joel Feinberg has pointed out, what we call a cause is often in fact not an individual, isolated event, but an event or state of affairs that is connected to others, thus forming a so-called 'causal context'. Any single element of such a causal context is not by itself sufficient to bring about the result; only in conjunction with the other elements of the causal context does it become a sufficient condition. Thus, for example, when we say that the cause of a fire was the cigarette someone threw away in a forest, we tacitly imply that other conditions without which the effect would not have come about (for instance, the presence of oxygen in the air) were satisfied too . When we say that someone's throwing away a cigarette was the cause of a fire instead of saying that the cause was, for instance, the presence of oxygen in the air, we individuate the former as an anomalous element of the respective context. What distinguishes an element as a cause and makes us pick it out from among the other conditions is its contextual anomality. But that anomality, in turn, depends on contextual circumstances. In a scientific experiment under artificially created laboratory

[7] Searle 1983, p. 80.

[8] For a summary of some theories of causality, cf. González Lagier 1994; on the idea of natural necessity, cf. von Wright 1971.

conditions, the undesired presence of oxygen may well be regarded as the cause of a fire.[9]

That dependence of the notion of cause on the respective context and the interests of the observer, however, does not mean that the relationship between a cause (embedded in the corresponding context) and an effect is not of a natural kind. After all, the 'causal force' of the context does not depend on the observer.

4.2. CONVENTIONAL RELATIONS

If the change in the world is an institutional change, the relation or link under scrutiny is a conventional or normative relation. Conventional relations are established by rules or conventions. If we want to draw a parallel between the natural and the normative world, we can perhaps say that in the normative world some rules occupy a place similar to that of causal laws in the natural world (but, of course, with that assertion I do not mean to deny that causal laws are descriptive: causal laws describe causal relations, whereas rules *create* or *constitute* conventional relations).

What kind of rules establish such conventional relations? Basically, they must be rules which link the 'occurrence' of a certain state of affairs (in our case, in the last instance, the performance of certain bodily movements under certain circumstances) to a particular normative change (that is, a change interpreted in the light of a system of rules). As we have seen in Chapter V, this applies to the rules Searle calls 'constitutive'. In the legal sphere, however, it is not always easy to distinguish constitutive from regulative rules. Thus, a norm stipulating a sanction for murder has traditionally been considered a regulative rather than a constitutive rule. But if no corresponding constitutive rule existed, we could not even speak of murder, nor would the respective institutional result ever come about. Hence, that norm also has a constitutive dimension.[10] Instead of looking for a criterion that would allow us to draw a sharp line between the two kinds of rules, we can therefore concede that rules (including regulative rules or rules of conduct) have a constitutive dimension. And it is these *rules with a constitutive dimension* which establish a conventional link between certain bodily movements and an institutional change.

4.3. RELATIONS OF IMPLICATION?

Under certain circumstances, to bring about one effect may 'imply' (in a very broad sense) to bring about another. Thus, under certain circumstances, to wake up implies to wake up early; to jump more than two meters implies to jump higher than George; to say something implies to lie; to kill John implies to take revenge, etc. In such cases, the two effects (or the two descriptions of one and the same change or effect) are linked by a relationship that is given by the respective context and by semantic rules, a

[9] Nagel 1961.

[10] Joseph Raz has therefore criticized Searle's distinction of regulative and constitutive rules. Cf. Raz 1990, pp. 108 ff.; also, González Lagier 1993.

relationship that is neither of a causal nor of a conventional nature in the sense just explained.[11]

Some authors have referred to a similar relationship between actions, saying that one action is a *version* of the other. Thus, according to Mosterín, „an action is a version of another when both actions have the same agent, are performed at the same time, and the event involved in the first implies the event involved in the second".[12] Eating a salad, for example, is a version of eating. I think it may be useful to stipulate that in such cases, to the extent that the relationship depends on the meaning of the terms used to refer to them, there are not two different changes or actions, but two descriptions (or versions) of one and the same change or action. From that point of view, only causal or conventional changes give rise to new actions.

5. Intention

Intention is, no doubt, the most complex element of action. Some of the problems the concept of intention poses come from the ambiguity of expressions such as 'intention', 'intentional action', and 'voluntary action'. Others involve longstanding philosophical questions (such as that of the relationship between mental and physical entities). In the following paragraphs, I will mention some distinctions and considerations which in my view are of special importance for an analysis of that notion.

5.1 INTENTIONALITY AND INTENTION

First of all, we must distinguish between intentionality as a feature of mental events (or the Intentionality of the mind, in general),[13] and intention as a feature of actions. For an understanding of that distinction, the following approach by Searle may be helpful:

„As a preliminary formulation we might say: Intentionality is that property of many mental states and events by which they are directed at or about or of objects and states of affairs in the world. If, for example, I have a belief, it must be a belief that such and such is the case; if I have a fear, it must be a fear of something or that something will occur; if I have a desire, it must be a desire to do something or that something should happen or be the case; if I have an intention, it must be an intention to do something."[14]

According to Searle, not all mental states and events have Intentionality („there are – he says – forms of nervousness, elation, and undirected anxiety that are not Intentional"[15]). If a state is Intentional, there must be an answer to questions such as 'About what?', 'Of

[11] This encompasses the cases Alvin Goldman has called 'simple generation' and 'augmentation generation'; cf. Chapter III, sect. 1.2.

[12] Mosterín 1983, p. 174.

[13] Searle proposes to write Intentionality or Intentional, with a capital 'I', when we refer to the intentionality of mental states in general.

[14] Searle 1983, p. 1.

[15] Ibid.

what?', etc. Thus, for instance, if someone informs me that he has a belief or a want, it makes sense to ask 'What is it you believe?' or 'What is it you want?', and the answer cannot be 'I just have a belief (a want), but without believing (wanting) anything'.

To have the intention to do something, or the intention that accompanies an action, is just another state of Intentionality (as in the case of wants or beliefs). Despite the terminological similarity, there is no reason why the intention linked to actions should play any special role in a theory of Intentionality; in other words, that a state is Intentional does not mean that it necessarily involves some kind of intention.[16]

In any case, to speak of mental states, and of intention as a mental state, is to take sides in the controversy about the existence of such states and in the corresponding action-theoretic discussion between volitionists and non-volitionists.

5.2 DO INTENTIONS EXIST IN THE MIND? VOLITIONISTS AND ANTI-VOLITIONISTS

We have seen that the concept of intention can be constructed as referring to a mental state or to the sense we attribute to an action according to certain rules and conventions.[17] These two ways of understanding the notion of intention can be linked to a more general discussion about the existence of 'volitions' as mental states.

The starting point of that discussion is the following:[18] on one understanding of 'voluntariness', an action is voluntary when the bodily movements that constitute it are caused by a mental phenomenon which is usually called 'will', 'volition', 'act of will', etc. According to that conception, all actions have an internal phase (the volition) and an external phase (the bodily movements and their consequences). If the internal phase is missing, or if there is no relation of causality between the internal and the external phase, then there is no voluntary action – in fact, there is no action at all. As we have already seen, this conception is known as the orthodox theory of action.[19] The assertion that there is such a thing as volitions is part of that theory.

The problem for 'volitionists' lies in the preconditions underlying their concept of 'voluntary action'. These preconditions are directly inherited from the philosophy of Descartes for whom the life of a human being takes place in two different, though parallel and interconnected worlds – the world of mind and the world of matter. The former is made up of a number of phenomena characterized by consciousness and temporal, but not spatial existence; the latter consists of those phenomena which exist in space and time and are material. Phenomena of the second kind are public in the sense that anyone can perceive them, whereas mental phenomena are strictly private because only oneself has access to them. There are interactions between the two kinds of phenomena, though it is difficult to say precisely what the nature of that connection is.[20]

[16] For a presentation of the problems posed by Intentionality and of different attempts to account for it, cf. Bechtel 1988, chs. 3 and 4.

[17] Cf., for example, Chapter IV, sect. 2.4.

[18] Here, I closely follow Nino's summary of the discussion, in Nino 1987, ch. III.

[19] Cf. Chapter IV, sect. 3.1.

[20] Simpson 1985, p. 57.

The Cartesian conception has been severely criticized by Ludwig Wittgenstein, Elizabeth Anscombe, and Gilbert Ryle, among others. Ryle has called it „the dogma of the Ghost in the Machine“ because it assumes that behind every action there is a ghost-like mental phenomenon that triggers it. Here are a few of Ryle's objections, concerning particularly the existence of volitions, as presented in his book *The Concept of Mind* (1949, ch. III):

(a) The predicates which apply to most events are inapplicable to volitions; in fact, ordinary language lacks terms to refer to them.

(b) We have no way of knowing directly what volitions others have; all valorations or explanations presupposing volitions are therefore based on mere conjectures.

(c) The nature of the causal relationships between volitions and bodily movements cannot be explained since the two kinds of phenomena have different ways of existence.

(d) If volitions are introduced in order to distinguish voluntary from involuntary actions, we must ask whether they are themselves voluntary or involuntary actions. If the answer is that they are voluntary actions, that leads to an infinite regress; if the answer is that they are involuntary, that answer seems absurd.

Others, such as A. I. Melden or H. L. A. Hart, have endorsed this kind of objections. The main problem of these critics is, however, that they should offer a satisfactory alternative to the alleged 'myth of volitions'. Thus, inspired by the later Wittgenstein, Ryle holds that many expressions referring to mental events (and the same is true, in his view, also in the particular case of volitions) simply denote behavioural dispositions, that is, they serve to speak about how someone behaves or how he is likely to behave. For example, we can explain what it means to say that someone believes that it will rain by indicating several propensities to act, such as taking an umbrella, cancelling the plans for a picknick, etc.[21] That conception, which can be regarded as a first manifestation of modern materialism, is known as philosophical or logical 'behaviourism'. The following passage by May Brodbeck which links that conception of mental states to the controversy about the adequate method for the humanities may help to clarify that position:

„Other people's mental states, their thoughts, feelings, wishes and hopes, are not directly accessible to public inspection. Nor can we test the everyday inferences we make to them, from what we do observe, in the same way that we can independently test, for instance, the inference from an observed change in color of a piece of litmus paper to a liquid's acidity. Though we frequently may be right in our everyday inferences to other people's mental states from their behavior, all we have to go on is what people choose to tell us or their observable behavior. Since there is no way of independently testing for the occurrence of these criteria and what they are criteria for, the proponents of a science of man eschew all talk about mental states. They maintain that nevertheless a complete description and causal explanation of human actions can be given *in principle* by means of terms that, like those of physical science, have reference only to objectively observable properties of material objects. The material objects of their concern are of course people's bodies, the characters, among others, are the observable behaviors of those bodies under certain conditions and in certain environments. The

[21] Bechtel 1988, ch. 5.

mentalistic terms characterising actions, like 'purpose' and 'thought', are, on this account, all eliminable by definitions using only nonmentalistic terms."[22]

Surely, the main enemy of behaviourism (to the extent that it is taken to be more than a methodological proposal) is common sense, because it denies something that seems intuitively obvious: I have intentions, beliefs, pains, sorrows, desires, fears, and hopes, and I experience them in ways which it seems very strange to explain in terms of propensities to act in this or that way. Behaviourists, however, dismiss the possibility that I may have access to my own mental states other than by external observation. That thesis has more than once been made fun of, with jokes like the following: A behaviourist says to another after making love 'It was great for you, how was it for me?'.[23] As Searle observes:

„Though perhaps most of the discussions in philosophical literature concern the 'technical' objections, in fact it is the common-sense objections that are the most embarrassing. The absurdity of behaviorism lies in the fact that it denies the existence of any inner mental states in addition to external behavior. And this, we know, runs dead counter to our ordinary experiences of what it is like to be a human being."[24]

Of course, that objection is not directed against all types of materialism, but only against those versions which deny the existence of mental states and of characteristics of these such as consciousness and Intentionality. Materialist theories that do not deny mental states leave the doors open for the explanation of voluntary actions as actions arising from volition. Some of the most renowned authors in the philosophy of action, such as Davidson and Goldman, have constructed their theories of action from a volitionist position (for them, volitions are a combination of desires and beliefs causally connected with actions) without committing themselves to the more conflictive aspects of dualism.

In fact, there seem to be good reasons for holding that what distinguishes (basic) actions from other bodily movements that do not constitute actions is that the former arise from a mental state which we can generically call 'will' or 'volition'. In order to underscore their difference from reflex-acts, such actions arising from the will are sometimes called 'voluntary actions'. But, as I said earlier, this is only one of the meanings of that expression.

5.3. INTENTIONS AND WANTS

What kind of mental states do we call 'volitions'? It seems that with this expression we refer basically to the wants and intentions of agents. Although they are often not distinguished (neither in ordinary language nor in specialized scholarship), the two states

[22] Brodbeck 1968, p. 59.

[23] Searle 1992, p. 35.

[24] Ibid.

have different features. According to Carlos Moya, a definition of intention should take into account the following differences between wants and intentions:[25]

(a) The objects of intentions are actions; they are intentions to perform this or that action; even when what we intend is to bring about a certain state of affairs, the *direct* object of intention is the action through which that state of affairs is produced. In contrast, besides actions, the content of wants may also be things, persons, or states of affairs. For instance, I may want a car, I may want to be tall, or I may want to go on a holiday; I may also have the intention to go on a holiday, but it makes no sense to say that I have the intention of a car or of being tall.

(b) While intentions do or do not affect an action as a whole, it is possible to feel a want and an aversion towards one and the same action, depending on which of its different aspects one looks at. As Moya writes: „One can adopt contrary attitudes, namely desires and aversions, towards the same thing, person, state of affairs or action, because of their different aspects, but nothing similar happens with intention: it is incoherent to have and not to have the intention to do one and the same action."[26]

(c) Intentions are an 'all-or-nothing' affair, whereas wants can come in degrees: we may feel weaker or stronger desires, but we cannot have weaker or stronger intentions. Sometimes, we say that we have a particularly firm intention, but Moya thinks that this involves a different sense of 'force', by which we refer to our greater or lesser disposition to change our intention: „If I have the intention to do A, and not B or C, I do not intend to do A 'more' than I intend to do B or C: I do not intend to do B or C at all. But it is perfectly natural to speak about desiring to do something more than to do something else."[27]

(d) Whereas I may want something I know I cannot get, I cannot have the intention to do something I know I cannot do (at least a minimum of hope is needed, and even then my intention might better be described as the intention to *attempt* to do that thing).

(e) The 'logic' of intentions differs from the 'logic' of wants. Thus, for example, I cannot rationally have the intention to perform two actions which I know to be incompatible; and if action *B* follows from action *A* and I am aware of that, I cannot have the intention to do *A* without the intention to do *B*; similarly, if I have the intention to do *B* and I know that *A* is the only means to do it, I cannot have the intention to do *B* without the intention to do *A*. It is obvious that the same does not apply to wants.

(f) The intentions of an agent are self-referential in the sense that I can genuinely only have the intention to do something myself (to say that I have the intention that *x* do something is an indirect way of saying that I have the intention of myself making *x* do that thing). In contrast, I may well have the genuine desire that *x* do something.

25 Moya 1990, pp. 136 and 137.

26 Ibid., p. 136.

27 Ibid., p. 137. However, that feature seems more controversial to me, because the greater or lesser disposition to change an intention could be seen as an indicator (among other things) of the intensity of my intention to do something.

To these differences indicated by Carlos Moya, we could add another which Moya particularly emphasizes and regards as the core of his notion of intention:

(g) An intention implies a stronger *commitment* to action than a want: „In having an intention, I commit myself to make (if I think I will be able) or to try to make (if I do not think I will able) its content true."[28]

This is a feature that has been pointed out by several authors. But it is difficult to determine the exact nature of that *commitment.* Should we say that in forming an intention an obligation to act in a certain way arises? Moya seems to see it in this way when he says that intentions are backed by reasons and that „intentions commit us to act by virtue of the force of those reasons we take into account in forming them".[29] But that may pose difficulties when the reasons behind our intentions are not good reasons (and it seems undeniable that sometimes we have intentions that are based on bad reasons, that is, on reasons which neither justify nor – sometimes – rationally explain the action). But in that case, why should we act on our intentions? An alternative position is that of von Wright. According to von Wright, the 'air of commitment' intentions seem to imply derives from the *concept* of intention itself; it is for conceptual reasons that if someone declares to have the intention to do *x* and then does not do it although nothing prevents him from it, either we doubt whether he really had that intention or we think that he has behaved in a strange or irrational way:

„It is essential, however, that for short periods of time intervals the reliability of the predictions [of behaviour from declarations of intention] should be high. This seems to be a feature of the way in which the *concepts* of intention, of the various epistemic attitudes, and of action are related to one another."[30]

„We must, I think, regard it as a 'conceptual impossibility', that is, as something contrary to the way in which these concepts function in our thinking, that persons habitually fail to manifest their intentions in behaviour and therefore accept it as a 'conceptual necessity' that having an intention for immediate action *normally* results in action being initiated."[31]

One way of understanding what it is to have an intention which helps to explain some of the differences between intentions and wants (at least, features *b* - *f* indicated above) has been suggested by Donald Davidson in his essay on 'Intending'. For Davidson, an intention is a wish to perform an action that differs from other desires about actions in that it implies a global – rather than merely a *prima facie* – judgment that a certain action is desirable in the light of all available reasons. An intention, we could say, is a desire to act *all things considered*:

[28] Ibid., p. 138.

[29] Ibid., p. 140.

[30] Von Wright 1983a, p. 43.

[31] Von Wright 1980, p. 54.

„[...] a judgement that something I think I can do, and that I think I see my way clear to doing, a judgement that such an action is desirable not only for one or another reason but in the light of all my reasons; a judgement like this is not a mere wish. It *is* an intention.“[32]

„[...] intending and wanting belong to the same genus of pro attitudes expressed by value judgements. Wants, desires, principles, prejudices, felt duties and obligations provide reasons for actions and intentions, and are expressed by prima facie judgements; intentions and the judgements that go with intentional actions are distinguished by their all-out or inconditional form.“[33]

But that characterization of intention poses a problem because it seems to suggest that intentions are the result of a process of deliberation and of weighing reasons and beliefs consciously performed by the agent prior to the action, and that does not seem to apply to all actions we call intentional.

5.4. Intention prior to action, and intention in acting

Not everything we do intentionally we do after a process of deliberation or of weighing reasons. Many actions we call intentional are not premeditated actions. When we go for a walk, for example, we not always decide first which way we will go, but we nevertheless walk intentionally. When we engage in conversation, we not always decide previously what we are going to say, but we still talk intentionally. When someone insults us and we punch him in the nose, we punch him intentionally, though we may not have formed the previous intention of punching him should he insult us.

Searle points out that there are two kinds of intentional actions we perform without previously forming the intention of doing so (although it may be doubted whether actions of the second kind are really intentional):

(1) actions that form part of a preconceived plan, i. e., subsidiary actions that depend on a more encompassing action performed on a prior intention: „For example, suppose I have a prior intention to drive to my office, and suppose as I am carrying out this prior intention I shift from second gear to third gear. Now I formed no prior intention to shift from second to third. When I formed my intention to drive to the office I never gave it a thought. Yet my action of shifting gears was intentional“;

(2) actions that are not part of any action performed on a prior intention or of a plan of life. For example, „suppose I am sitting in a chair reflecting on a philosophical problem, and I suddenly get up and start pacing about the room. My getting up and pacing about are clearly intentional actions, but in order to do them I do not need to form an intention to do them prior to doing them“.[34]

Some authors try to account for the intentional nature of such actions by asserting that the intention to perform these actions is an unconscious intention. Thus, for Carlos Moya, for example, intentions to perform a future action are not necessarily „conscious

[32] Davidson 1980d, p. 101.

[33] Ibid., p. 102.

[34] Searle 1983, p. 85.

mental episodes".[35] But there seems to be something strange about the idea of an unconscious intention (although our intentions may well come in different degrees of consciousness). Other authors introduce a distinction between two kinds of intentions. For example, Searle distinguishes between *prior intentions* and *intentions in action*. When we say that we punched someone in the nose intentionally, but without having formed the intention to do it, what we want to say is that we did not have the prior intention to do it, but that the action was therefore no less intentional. Searle proposes the following criterion for distinguishing between the two kinds of intentions:

„The characteristic linguistic form of expression of a prior intention is 'I will do *A*' or 'I am going to do *A*'. The characteristic form of expression of an intention in action is 'I am doing *A*'. We say of a prior intention that the agent acts on his intention, or that he carries out his intention, or that he tries to carry it out; but in general we can't say such things of intentions in action, because the intention in action just is the Intentional content of the action; the action and the intention are inseparable [...]"[36]

Now, the question that is still pending is: Are intentions *in action* mental states? Are they in the mind?

5.5. INTERNAL (SUBJECTIVE) INTENTION AND EXTERNAL (OBJECTIVE) INTENTION

Perhaps the problem raised by intention *in action* shows that even if we choose the volitionist alternative in order to construct the notion of 'intention', we also need a concept of intention that owes something to the non-mentalists.

Recall that, according to the volitionists themselves, intentions (and mental states in general) are strictly private, in the sense that we have no access to the intentions of others; at best, we can infer what seem to be their intentions from their conduct, comparing it with our standards of expectation. Not even by asking an agent can we learn something beyond all doubt about his intentions, because the answer is itself an action regarding which we can again ask with what intention it was performed.

The fact that ascribing a particular intention to an agent is the result of an inference from the observation of his conduct may lead one to think that the concept of intention we are interested in is not a concept that refers to the individual's mental state – that intention is not in the individual's mind, but that it is something *in the action* (or, more specifically, in the circumstances and the context of the action) which enables me to draw that inference (or that it is the result of that inference, i. e., what in the next section I will call the intentional interpretation of an action). That is a way of understanding the concept of intention that comes very close to that of the behaviourists.[37] In that sense, some authors have suggested that „there are two models for intention, in one of which there is an internal psychological element which an angel could discover and

[35] Moya 1990, p. 132.

[36] Searle 1983, p. 85.

[37] Which, as we have seen, is said to be the notion underlying the social theory of action of criminal-law doctrine as well as the ascriptive theory of H. L. A. Hart.

in the other a coherent pattern of external behaviour".[38] With respect to these ideas, we can speak of 'internal intention' and 'external intention', or of 'intention in the subjective sense' and 'intention in the objective sense'. Now, what I want to suggest is that Searle's notion of 'intention in action' can be understood in the sense of 'external intention'. When we speak of intentional actions performed without a prior intention, what we probably mean is that such actions can be explained in teleological terms and that, although in fact no deliberation preceded their performance, if we had weighed our reasons for action we would have performed them just the same. What we want to say is that the observation of such an action allows us to infer an intention although there has not really been a prior intention, i. e., that we can give an intentional interpretation of the action in the light of existing circumstances and our knowledge of the world. We therefore say that there was an intention *in action.*

I think, however, that the external or objective sense of intention is secondary to the internal or subjective sense. As we have seen, the external sense of intention, i. e., the intentional interpretation of action, can be applied to actions performed with a prior intention as well as to actions performed without such an intention. In the former case, it does indeed depend on the respective prior intention: if we could have exact knowledge of the intention, understood as a mental state of the agent, our intentional interpretation of his conduct should basically not differ from his own. In other words, what we try to infer from the observation of his conduct is precisely what his internal intention prior to the action was. In the latter case, in contrast, when there is no prior intention (i. e., when there is an action we call 'intentional', but which has been performed without previous deliberation), the intentional interpretation, the intention *in acting*, or external intention, depends on the prior intention the agent *would* have had if he had stopped to deliberate before acting, and on the explanation he can give of his conduct.

I therefore think that we can conclude that, just as in some actions the element of change in the world may overlap with the bodily movements, there are also other actions where the element of intention overlaps with the requirement of the interpretation of the action.

5.6. VOLUNTARINESS AND INTENTION

To conclude these conceptual considerations about the notion of intention, it may be useful to attempt to clarify the relationship between voluntary and intentional action.

As mentioned before, it is sometimes said that an action is voluntary when it has been caused by the agent's will. Sometimes, however, the distinction between voluntary and involuntary action has nothing to do with the question whether or not there is a corresponding will, or a causal relationship between such a will and an action. On some occasions, for instance, we say that an action was voluntary merely in order to say that it was not obligatory, that it was performed on one's own, without any kind of coercion; on others, we say that an action was involuntary in the sense of unintended ('My action of alerting the enemy by lighting a match was involuntary, I only meant to light a ciga-

[38] White 1985, p. 72; White presents that thesis without adopting it himself.

rette'[39]). I think that an adequate approach to a systematic account of some of the senses of the expression 'voluntary action' and its contrary, and of their relations to 'intentional action' is to analyze them in the light of the distinction between basic act, result-act and consequence-act.

(a) When we speak of 'action' in the sense of 'basic act', 'voluntary action' can only mean the existence of a causal relationship between a volition of the agent and his bodily movements. That is the sense of 'voluntariness' we use when we say that what distinguishes actions from mere bodily movements is their voluntariness (sometimes, 'intentionality' is also used in that same sense). Basic acts are always voluntary. An involuntary action is an action where the volition or the causal connection is missing. The bodily movement may then have been produced by some external physical force (as when someone else lifts my arm) or mental force (other than the will), or in a state of unconsciousness. Sometimes it is said that such occurrences are not actions in the proper sense.

(b) When we speak of 'action' in the sense of 'result-act', 'voluntary action' may be equivalent to 'intentional action', that is, it may refer to an action that is in accordance with the agent's intention or will. Sometimes, however, we also say that an intentional action was involuntary – for example, because it is legally obligatory, or because it has been performed under a threat or some other kind of coercion, or in a state of emergency, or because there simply was no alternative. Such actions are voluntary in the first sense (they arise from a volition), and they are also intentional (in the sense that they are interpreted on the basis of the agent's intention).

(c) Finally, when we understand 'action' in the sense of 'consequence-act', we can say that an action is voluntary, but unintentional, that is, that it is an undesired consequence of some other, intentional action. 'Voluntary' then means 'consequence of an intentional action'. According to our definition of consequence-acts, they are all voluntary in that sense. Only if we broaden our concept of action to include reflex-acts, we can speak of involuntary consequence-acts in reference to the consequences of reflex-acts.

Hence, there are at least three different senses of 'voluntariness' (as distinguished from 'intentionality'), corresponding to the three senses of 'action'. A voluntary basic act is a basic act rooted in a volition; a voluntary result-act is a result-act that is performed freely (without coercion), in the presence of possible alternative actions (including omission); and a voluntary consequence-act is a consequence of an intentional act which is not itself intentional.

6. The Interpretation or Meaning of an Action

6.1. WHAT DOES 'MEANING OF AN ACTION' MEAN?

There is a passage in Wittgenstein which seems to be an obligatory reference for all works on the theory of action, and this is the moment for me to comply with that tradi-

[39] Nino 1987, p. 36.

tion: „what is left over if I subtract the fact that my arm goes up from the fact that I raise my arm?“[40] Many philosophers have thought that the correct answer to this question is that 'what is left over' when we subtract the bodily movement from an action is the *meaning* of that movement. But it is far from obvious what the expression 'the meaning of an action' means. Moreover, the question about the meaning of 'meaning' is an extremely difficult and complex question to answer. Part of that difficulty derives from the fact that 'meaning' too is an ambiguous word. C. K. Ogden and I. A. Richards, for instance, have distinguished sixteen different senses in which the word is used.[41] Now, what can we say about the meaning of an action?

This is one of the questions around which part of the debate about the distinction between the natural and the human sciences have revolved. It has been said that what is characteristic of the human sciences is precisely the study of phenomena that have a sense or meaning, which makes it impossible to account for them in purely causal terms. The controversy about the proper method of the human sciences and their distinction from the natural sciences can be seen, as von Wright suggests, as the continuation of two traditions concerning the model of explanation in science: the Galilean tradition (which sees the task of science in causal explanation) and the Aristotelian tradition (which sees it in teleological explanation). According to J. M. Mardones, these two traditions have until today been replicated in several pairs of opposing currents, such as 19th-century positivism *versus* hermeneutics; Russell's and the early Wittgenstein's logical positivism and Popper's critical rationalism *versus* Critical Theory (Adorno, Habermas); positions upholding the applicability to action of the model of explanation based on subsumption to general laws (the deductive-nomological model) *versus* those emphasizing the role of intentions or different language games; and, finally, theories focusing on logical and normative models (Lakatos) *versus* those underscoring the social and historical nature of science (Kuhn).[42]

An analysis of the Aristotelian tradition and its different versions through history suggests that there are basically two possible candidates for what 'the meaning of an action' may consist of. One possibility is that we relate the question of the meaning of an action to its *teleological explanation*, that is, that we understand an action when we can answer the question 'Why or what for did *x* do *y*?'; the other possibility is to say that we understand an action or that we know its meaning when we can answer the question 'What is *y*?'. These two questions lead us to the distinction between *explaining* and *understanding* a conduct.[43]

40 Wittgenstein 1958, § 621.

41 Ogden/Richards 1923, pp. 186 f.

42 Mardones 1991.

43 The distinction between explanation and understanding is usually characterized in more suggestive, but at the same time more vague terms. I here adopt the distinction drawn by Georg Henrik von Wright. For von Wright, the difference between the two types of sciences should not be understood as based on the difference between 'explaining' and 'understanding', but between *intentional or teleological* explanation and understanding, on the part of the human sciences, and *causal or functional* explanation, on the part of the natural sciences. Cf. von Wright 1971, esp. the last chapter.

Jon Elster seems to have the first candidate in mind when he says:

„In everyday life – in politics, in the family or at the work-place – one constantly encounters the implicit assumption that any social or psychological phenomenon must have a meaning or significance that explains it: there must be some sense or some perspective in which it is beneficial for someone or something -- and these benefits also explain the presence of the phenomenon."[44]

For Elster, the meaning of an action is what allows us to explain that action, what makes it rational in the light of certain objectives. From this point of view, the meaning of an action is linked to intention, to the aim or purpose pursued by the agent. „The meaning of an action", Mosterín likewise observes, „is the end the agent pursues with it"; and he adds: „The interpretation of an action is the answer to the question about the sense of that action."[45]

The other alternative – that we comprehend the meaning of an action when we *understand* the action – is what von Wright opts for when he presents the distinction between teleological explanation and understanding.[46] To understand an action is to answer the question 'What is action *y*?', that is, it consists in *classifying* the conduct or bodily movements we observe as a particular type of action, in subsuming it under a certain class of actions. The process of interpreting an action is, from this perspective, a process of classifying an individual action under a generic class of actions.

Now, despite the distinction between teleological explanation and understanding, explanations based on an agent's intentions and the interpretation or understanding of a conduct are closely related. On the one hand, in order to explain why a particular agent performed some action *x*, I must first determine what kind of action it is, i. e., I must interpret the action as such-and-such an action. On the other hand, in order to interpret an action it is useful (and for some actions it is the only feasible way) to know the agent's intentions, i. e., to have knowledge about that which explains why that agent performed that action.[47]

If one contends that the meaning of an action is what explains it as rational, that is, that the meaning of an action is the purpose pursued with it (or, still more precisely, the purpose the agent in question pursues with it), then the problem is that we cannot speak of the meaning of unintentional actions. Such actions would be meaningless. In contrast, to regard the meaning of an action as that which allows one to classify or understand it as an action of a particular kind is „a broader meaning of meaning" (because it also encompasses unintentional actions). I will therefore understand the expression 'meaning of an action' in the latter sense and speak of the interpretation of an action as the process of looking for its meaning, that is, of subsuming a particular individual action under some class of actions. The expression 'interpretation of an action' can refer to that same process, or to its result.

[44] Elster 1983, p. 101.

[45] Mosterín 1983, pp. 182 and 186.

[46] Von Wright 1971, p. 134.

[47] Ibid., pp. 132 ff.

Obviously, this sense of meaning is not the same as linguistic meaning. Only actions with a communicative purpose also have a linguistic meaning.

Now, what is it that makes us subsume a bodily movement under a particular class of actions? I think in most cases the answer is the following: we classify a bodily movement as an action of bringing about a certain change (in the weak or strong sense, and of a natural or institutional kind). The class of actions under which we subsume a bodily movement depends on that change. Hence, the process of interpreting an action can be seen as the process of choosing the 'action-internal change' from the chain of changes initiated by the movement.

As already indicated in Chapter V, 'pragmatics' in a general sense can be understood as the study of „how we *ascribe meaning to our actions*, when we perform them, *or to the actions of others*, when we understand them“.[48] The ideal objective of pragmatics therefore is to spell out the 'grammar' (in a very wide sense) of actions (not only of speech acts), that is, to determine the set of principles and criteria according to which we attribute a certain sense to actions, interpret them in one way or the other. Perhaps that goal cannot be reached. It seems to be accessible only for action in institutional contexts (including speech acts). I will here content myself with some observations relating to that process of interpretation. Perhaps a convenient way to proceed is to start with the so-called inferential model of language and extend it to other actions.[49]

6.2. THE INTENTIONAL INTERPRETATION OF BODILY MOVEMENTS

6.2.1. For the inferential model of language, according to Bustos, „the main pillar of the pragmatic explanation of the production of meaning is an inference concerning communicative intentions: the speaker infers the adequate means of his utterance from his communicative intentions, given his knowledge of the situation, and from what the speaker does the audience infers the speaker's communicative intention, what he meant to say“.[50] Bustos also presents a simple model of the production of meaning, featuring three aspects or stages:[51]

(a) The agent has the purpose of transmitting a certain information to a receiver or audience.

(b) He therefore brings into play his knowledge of the set of conventions and procedures which, since they are shared by the communication community to which both the receiver and the agent himself belong, allow the latter to express that meaning.

(c) The agent uses those procedures according to his knowledge of the *situation* in which he will perform the action; that knowledge basically constitutes what is known

48 Bustos 1997, p. 294.

49 Cf. Chapter V, sect. 1.

50 Bustos 1997, p. 267.

51 Ibid., p. 268.

as the *context* of the speech act and determines at least partly the meaning of the action that is performed.

Bustos concludes that the agent's inference has the following form: 'If I want to say *x*, then, given *C*, I must do *z*', where *x* is the object of the agent's communicative intention, *C* is the context, and *z* the speech act.

This is a valid pattern for speech acts, which, at least in central cases, are institutional and intentional actions. Now we must ask whether there is a possibility to extend this model to other, institutional as well as natural, intentional actions. In my view, this requires the following modification of the model:

(a') The agent wants to bring about a (natural or institutional) change *x*, as the result of his action.

(b') He therefore brings into play his knowledge of the set of technical rules, either natural (based on causal laws) or institutional (based on conventions of a constitutive nature) which allow him to bring about that change.

(c') The agent uses those technical rules according to his knowledge of the context in which he will perform the action.

The agent's inference will then be as follows: 'If I want to bring about result *x* (that is, perform action *x*), then, given *C*, I must make bodily movements *z*', and the inference of an interpreting observer: 'If he has done the bodily movements *z*, then, given *C*, he had the intention of (performing the action of) bringing about *x*'.

This model explains how the agent makes sense of his action. Since it is the agent himself who gives that intentional meaning to it, the question 'How do you know that you have done *x*?' makes no sense. Strictly speaking, an agent does not interpret his own actions; rather, he gives meaning to them and therefore *knows* what meaning they have.

6.2.2. When an observer tries to interpret bodily movements, in contrast, certain difficulties arise since it is impossible to have direct access to another's mind. The inference 'If he has done bodily movements *z*, then, given *C*, he had the intention of (performing the action of) bringing about *x*' is based (among other things) on the following factors:

(i) knowledge of certain causal relationships, that is, of the adequate causal means for reaching certain natural ends;

(ii) knowledge of constitutive rules, that is, of the adequate conventional means for reaching certain institutional ends;

(iii) knowledge of the social habits of behaviour and the rules of a regulative kind accepted by the agent; and

(iv) knowledge of the agent's character and personality.

Besides, there is a number of principles regarding intention which can guide us in the intentional interpretation of an action:

(α) If I have the intention to do *A*, and I know that *B* is incompatible with *A*, then I do not have the intention to do *B*.

(β) If action *B* obviously follows from action *A*, I cannot have the intention to do *A* without also having the intention to do *B*.

(γ) If I have the intention to do *B*, and I know that *A* is the only means for it, I cannot have the intention to do *B* without also having the intention to do *A*.

In my view, these principles do not describe necessary characteristics of intention; rather, they constitute defeasible presumptions about the intention of people under certain circumstances.[52] They help an observer to put himself in the agent's shoes and interpret his action, but they do not guarantee that the interpretation is correct. The intentional interpretation an observer gives the bodily movements of another agent does not necessarily coincide with the agent's actual intention although it should attempt to approach that goal as closely as possible.

6.2.3. This last assertion is connected with a feature of mental attitudes such as believing, desiring, having an intention, knowing, etc. These mental (or, in the terminology of philosophers of language, propositional) attitudes give rise to 'opaque' (or 'oblique', or 'intensional') contexts. Opaque contexts are an exception to Leibniz's Principle of Substitutibility, according to which in any context we can substitute one expression for another with the same reference without altering the truth-value of the sentence to which it belongs.[53] Thus, for example, from 'Lois Lane believes that Superman is daring' it does not follow that 'Lois Lane believes that Clark Kent is daring' (even if Superman and Clark Kent are the same person). Similarly, as we already know, from 'Oedipus intended to marry Jocasta' it does not follow that 'Oedipus intended to marry his mother'. There are many explanations for this phenomenon. Concerning mental states, perhaps the most suggestive is the one saying that beliefs, desires, intentions, etc. do not refer to objects of reality, but to propositions or mental representations.[54] If that is so, what satisfies an intention is not an action or change in the world, but a certain version, description or interpretation of that action or change. Thus, for example, suppose Alfred has the intention to jump higher than two metres, and that John has not jumped higher than a metre and a half. What satisfies Alfred's intention is not jumping higher than John, but jumping higher than two metres, even though 'jumping higher than John' and 'jumping higher than two metres' can be different versions or descriptions of one and the same natural change. Would we say that in this case the action of 'jumping higher than John' is intentional?

I think that the question about the degree of divergence we admit between an intention and an intentional interpretation of a bodily movement cannot be decided with-

[52] The plausibility of these presumptions derives, on the one hand, from our experience and, on the other, from the notion of intention (just as, according to von Wright, the fact that an intention implies a commitment to the corresponding action is due to the concept of intention itself). Cf. above, sect. 5.3.

[53] Cf. García Suárez 1997, p. 253.

[54] Cf. ibid., pp. 278 ff.

out taking into account considerations about the interest we have in the interpretation of an action. General criteria can therefore hardly be given.

6.3. THE NON-INTENTIONAL INTERPRETATION OF BODILY MOVEMENTS

The inferential model of language can offer useful guidance only for intentional actions because it assumes that the agent's intention is inferred from his conduct. When we ask about the meaning of non-intentional actions, we must focus not on the agent, but on the circumstances and conventions involved in the performance of the respective bodily movement. Since we have characterized non-intentional actions as consequence-acts, a non-intentional action is an unintended consequence of an intentional action (or result-act). Probably all intentional actions have consequences, but not all of these can be regarded as action-internal changes, that is, not all consequences of an intentional action can be used to attribute to the agent the action of giving rise to that change (even if one can recognize that the agent *caused* that change). But which consequences these are is a question related more to the ascriptive or attributive function of language than to a descriptive function.[55]

The non-intentional interpretation of bodily movements is guided by certain criteria which have a double function: on the one hand, they 'authorize' us to switch from an intentional interpretation to an interpretation of bodily movements that does not take an agent's intention into account; on the other, they allow us to determine which consequence of the chain of changes initiated by the bodily movements we can pick out to attribute a non-intentional action to the agent.

As Ricardo Guibourg has observed, it is very difficult to classify the criteria for the individuation of actions; besides, rather than making individuation *decidable*, they only operate as motivations of variable strength and must be weighed against each other. In his view, the most obvious criteria (besides intention) are the following:[56]

(a) the length of the chain of effects: the farther away from the basic act or bodily movement a consequence is, the weaker our disposition to identify it with an action that can be attributed to the agent;

(b) predictability: the more predictable a consequence is (or should be) for the agent, the more disposed we are to attribute the corresponding action to him or her;

(c) the intervention of another basic act (or any kind of event that strengthens the chain of consequences): „If between the First Event [my 'basic act'] and the Second Event [my 'consequence'] there appears some other fact that could be identified as a First Event different from the former, we tend to cut off the causal chain, in tribute to the doctrine of free will“[57];

(d) social relevance: the more relevant the consequence in question, the more disposed we are to accept a greater extension of the chain.

[55] On these questions, cf. Chapter VI, sect. 1.4.

[56] Guibourg 1987, pp. 49 ff.

[57] Ibid., p. 53.

The social relevance of a consequence is, of course, relative to a system of rules. Here, we must again distinguish between a system's regulative and its constitutive rules (or its rules with a constitutive dimension). Either type can indicate that a change is relevant. For example, bringing about a change that is prohibited by a regulative rule is a socially relevant event. And the fact that a change is stipulated in a rule with a constitutive dimension as a precondition for the production of a normative result also gives relevance to that change.[58]

One last criterion related to that of social relevance could be added to the list: sometimes, the fact that a change was brought about in a justified way prevents that a corresponding action is attributed to an agent. For example, if I kill someone in legitimate self-defense, an action of killing, but not an action of murder will be attributed to me. There is a conventional connection between killing and murdering. Justifications (but not excuses) sever that conventional connection.

[58] Concerning non-intentional actions or consequence-acts, the only function of constitutive rules is that they facilitate the interpretation of the meaning of an action; but, in contrast to what is the case concerning result-acts, they do not have the function of allowing the agent intentionally to perform a new kind of action.

CHAPTER VIII

OTHER KINDS OF ACTIONS

1. Introduction

The previous chapters have offered some tools for a better understanding of the concept of action. On the one hand, we have encountered three senses of the term 'action' (basic act, result-act, and consequence-act), and we have seen that each one of them refers to one of the dimensions actually present in an action. From that perspective, actions are a complex phenomenon that cannot adequately be reconstructed if one of these dimensions (the natural, the subjective, and the objective) is ignored. On the other hand, we have analyzed five elements to be found in many cases of action (bodily movements, changes in the world, a link between the two, intention, and interpretation). To complete the presentation, in this chapter I will use these tools to formulate a few brief observations about two particular kinds of actions, to wit, institutional actions and omissions.

2. Institutional Actions

2.1. JOHN SEARLE'S DISTINCTION BETWEEN NATURAL AND INSTITUTIONAL ACTIONS

Several authors have introduced the distinction between natural and institutional actions. One of the classical passages concerning this distinction can be found in John Searle's *Speech Acts*. Searle writes:

„There is a certain picture we have of what constitutes the world and consequently of what constitutes knowledge about the world. The picture is easy to recognize but hard to describe. It is a picture of the world as consisting of brute facts, and of knowledge as really knowledge of brute facts. [... It is thought] that the concepts which make up the knowledge are essentially physical, or, in its dualistic version, either physical or mental. The model for systematic knowledge of this kind is the natural sciences, and the basis for all knowledge of this kind is generally supposed to be simple empirical observations recording sense experiences. [... But] there are many kinds of facts, and facts which obviously are objective facts and not matters of opinion or sentiment or emotion at all, which are hard, if not impossible, to assimilate to this picture.“[1]

Searle mentions the following examples of facts that cannot be reduced to brute facts: getting married, winning a soccer game, approving an appointment in Parliament, etc. And he adds that

[1] Searle 1969, pp. 50 f.

„there is no simple set of statements about physical or psychological properties of states of affairs to which the statements of facts such as these are reducible".[2]

Although such facts may include some variety of brute physical movements, states and sensations, a description of these facts in 'brute' terms is always insufficient since their complete meaning can be understood only with reference to institutions. That is, their existence presupposes the existence of certain institutions (that is why Searle calls them 'institutional facts') which Searle understands as systems of constitutive rules.[3] Hence, the existence of institutional facts (and institutional actions, which Searle regards as a kind of facts) definitely depends on constitutive rules:

„imagine what it would be like to describe institutional facts in purely brute terms. Let us imagine a group of highly trained observers describing an American football game in statements only of brute facts. What could they say by way of description? Well, within certain areas a good deal could be said, using statistical techniques certain 'laws' could even be formulated. For example, we can imagine that after a time our observer would discover the law of periodical clustering: at statistically regular intervals organisms in like colored shirts cluster together in a roughly circular fashion (the huddle). Furthermore, at equally regular intervals, circular clustering is followed by linear clustering (the teams line up for the play), and linear clustering is followed by the phenomenon of linear interpenetration. Such laws would be statistical in character, and none the worse for that. But no matter how many data of this sort we imagine our observers to collect and no matter how many inductive generalizations we imagine them to make from the data, they still have not described American football. What is missing from their description? What is missing are all those concepts which are backed by constitutive rules, concepts such as touchdown, offside, game, points, first down, time out, etc., and consequently what is missing are all the true statements one can make about a football game using those concepts [...] institutional facts can only be explained in terms of the constitutive rules which underlie them."[4]

2.2. TWO KINDS OF INSTITUTIONAL ACTIONS

Searle's characterization of institutional actions is aimed at explaining the connection between constitutive rules and speech acts. The only institutional actions he is interested in are speech acts. But if we apply our conceptual tools to this topic, we can discern two kinds of institutional actions.

We can characterize the distinction between natural actions and institutional actions as follows (leaving aside basic acts, which are always natural actions):

Natural actions

(a) are result-acts or consequence-acts and
(b) bring about a natural change, i. e., a change independent of rules, where
(c) the relationship between the bodily movements and that change is a causal relationship.

Institutional actions

(a) are result-acts or consequence-acts and

[2] Ibid., p. 51.

[3] Cf. Chapter V, sect. 5.2, and Chapter VII, sect. 4.2.

[4] Searle 1969, p. 52.

(b) bring about an institutional change, i. e., a change depending on rules with a constitutive dimension, where

(c) the relationship between the bodily movements and that change is, in some stretch, a conventional relationship.

Institutional result-acts differ from institutional consequence-acts in that in order for the former to come about it is necessary that the agent has the intention to bring about the institutional effect by using the corresponding constitutive rule. Searle's speech acts are a clear example of this, but so are institutional actions such as getting married, pronouncing a sentence, dictating a law, etc. In such actions, the agent's intention and the conventional means at his disposition for bringing about the result are intertwined. And that close link implies that, on the one hand, if the intention is missing the conventional result does not come about, and, on the other, if the procedure stipulated in the rule is followed, there is a strong presumption that the agent did have the intention to bring about the conventional effect. Institutional consequence-acts, in contrast, are imputed to an agent regardless of whether or not he had the intention to bring about the institutional effects. In other words, while in institutional result-acts the agent necessarily uses the constitutive rule to bring about a certain result foreseen in that rule, in institutional consequence-acts the agent does not normally use the constitutive rule, and the result, in any case, is brought about regardless of whether or not he does. That is the case, for example, of torts and crimes.[5]

We can thus account for the difference between what civil lawyers call declarations of will or legal acts (which are institutional result-acts) and legal facts in the strict sense (which are actually not facts – understood as something entirely independent of the human will – but institutional consequence-acts).[6]

3. Remarks on Omission

Finally, I will now contrast the structure of actions with that of omissions. My starting point will be the broader notion of omission according to which it consists in not doing something one could or should have done, or at least was expected to do.[7] That notion, however, is located at the upper end of a scale of definitions of omission of varying strength. Thus, in *Norm and Action* von Wright offers the following definitions:

„On our definition, forbearing to do something which one can do does not presuppose *awareness* of the opportunity. In a stronger sense of 'forbear', an agent forbears only such action as he knows he can perform on the occasion in question. In a still stronger sense, an agent forbears only such action as he knows he can perform but *decides* (chooses, prefers) to leave undone on the occasion in question. If, in addition, he feels an inclination or temptation to do the action, which he chooses not to do, then he is in a still stronger sense forbearing it."[8]

[5] When we say that a crime is intentional, what we actually want to say is that the natural action giving rise to the crime is intentional, not that there was an intention to bring about a crime.

[6] Cf. Chapter I, sect. 2.

[7] Cf., e. g., Nino 1987, p. 96.

[8] Von Wright 1963a, p. 46.

And in a later text, he presents the definition which I will adopt here:

„On most occasions there are innumerable things which I could do then but which I do not do simply because it does not occur to me to do them [...] Normally we should not say that I omitted to do these things then. But if I had a *reason* for doing or was *expected* to do some of the things, for example because it was my duty or because I had promised to, then we may say that I omitted what I did not do.“[9]

3.1. OMISSION AND BODILY MOVEMENTS

Let us first look at the relationship of omissions to the first of the elements of action, that is, bodily movements. According to the previous definitions, the characteristic feature of an omission is a 'not-doing'. But that does not necessarily imply that the subject is not performing any bodily movement when omitting something. It is perfectly possible (and even normal) that we omit an action while performing another one. For example, we can omit to turn off the tap of the bathtub while preparing dinner. What I mean when I say that an omission is a 'not-doing' is that an omission always implies the absence of the bodily movement that would be appropriate for performing a particular expected action, not the absence of any bodily movement at all.

Some philosophers, among them John Mackie,[10] as well as some criminal lawyers,[11] have argued that there is no such thing as omissions in reality, that speaking of an omission is rather only a particular way of describing a positive action. On this view, an omission is nothing but a negative aspect of an actual, positive act. When we say that someone omitted to turn off the tap, we would only be describing some other action, for example, that of preparing dinner. I think, however, that this view takes the compatibility of omissions with bodily movements too far, since, although it is true that we often do omit one thing while doing another, one can also imagine cases where we omit something while being absolutely at rest, in a state of bodily passivity. I can, for instance, omit to turn off the tap of the above-mentioned bathtub while laying in bed looking at the ceiling without doing anything. And if there are omissions the substrate of which is bodily passivity rather than a bodily movement, then omissions are not merely a kind of action description (since actions always presuppose bodily movement).

What we can assert, however, is that we have encountered a relevant difference between actions and omissions: whereas actions consist of interpreted bodily movements, omissions may consist either of interpreted bodily movements or of interpreted bodily passivity. The feature all omissions share is the absence of the particular bodily movement that would be appropriate to perform some expected action.

Now, if what is relevant in omissions is the absence of some bodily movement, can we say that omissions are, like actions, partly natural phenomena, 'anchored in the real world'? In my view, the answer to that question must be affirmative (the absence of a bodily movement is just as natural a phenomenon as, for example, the absence of rain

[9] Von Wright 1983b, pp. 109 f.

[10] On this point in Mackie, cf. Nino 1987, p. 115.

[11] On this conception of omission in criminal law and a critique, cf. Rodríguez Mourullo 1966, pp. 20 ff.

for a longer stretch of time).[12] I think that the reluctance to regard negative phenomena as part of the world has something to do with the difficulty to determine whether such phenomena can bring about effects, that is, whether there can be a causal relationship between them and a change in the world. That is a question I will come back to later.

3.2. OMISSION AND CHANGES IN THE WORLD

One might think that omissions also contain a change in the world as one of their elements – just like actions, though with some modifications. The change that is internal to an omission would be the contrary of the change that was expected or should have been brought about. If we speak of the omission of closing a door, the change internal to that omission would be that the door remains open, and the change internal to the corresponding action would be that the door is closed. In order to be able to speak of changes where what actually happens is that there is no transformation of the world at all, von Wright adopts the following definition: a change or event is the passage from one state of affairs to another or to *the same* state of affairs. But sometimes the change internal to an omission is a change in the narrow sense – for example, if we omit to prevent the door from being shut (e. g., by a draught of air).

3.3. OMISSION AND LINKS

Another question is whether there is some link between the absence of a bodily movement and the changes brought about in the world. In the case of actions, the relationship between a bodily movement and a change may be causal or conventional. But can there be a conventional relationship between the absence of a bodily movement and a change in the world? Or a causal connection? The answer to the first question concerns what criminal lawyers call 'omissions proper' (where what is punished is not having done a certain action, regardless of the consequences the omission may have had), whereas the answer to the second question concerns what they call cases of 'commission by omission' (where what is punished is having brought about a prohibited result by an omission).[13]

In omissions, the possibility of a conventional connection produces no problems. A convention or rule can stipulate that the absence of certain bodily movements has a normative result; it can stipulate, for example, that not to lift one's arm under certain circumstances counts as a vote against a proposal. That is what happens in the above-mentioned 'omissions proper', where it does not matter whether or not some natural result is brought about as a consequence of the omission. When one does not perform the bodily movements that could save someone in distress, one commits a violation by

[12] Someone might say that though the absence of a bodily movement is a natural phenomenon, the interpretation of such an absence as an omission is not; but the same applies to actions: giving an interpretation or meaning to a bodily movement (or to the absence of a bodily movement) is a fact that occurs in the social world.

[13] That kind of omission raises the problem of whether, in the words of George Fletcher, „crimes defined by action verbs such as killing, burning, maiming, assaulting and raping can be committed by people who stand and let events run their course" (Fletcher 1998, p. 46).

omission of the duty of assistance, which implies that certain legal consequences are produced.

A causal relationship between the absence of bodily movements and a natural change is more difficult to account for. That is the reason for the controversy in criminal law about the possibility of committing a crime by omission. What one can assert, however, is the possibility of causal relations of that kind, with a conception of causality as the one presented in section 4.1. of Chapter VII. If one accepts that theory of causality (which distinguishes the relationship between a causal context and an effect, on the one hand, from the selection of some element of that context as the cause, on the other), it seems that there are no relevant differences between bodily movements and the absence of bodily movements, as far as their possibility to constitute the cause of an effect is concerned. The anormal element of a context may be a bodily movement as well as its absence. Hence, we can say, for example, that my forgetting to put antifreeze in the engine was the cause for its getting wrecked, given the remaining circumstances, such as that the temperature dropped below zero, that water freezes at that temperature, etc. In the words of Ernesto Garzón Valdés: „When an omission completes the set of necessary conditions for the production of an event, thus making it sufficient, it is just as much a cause as an action that initiates a causal chain.“[14] Thus, the link between the absence of a bodily movement and a change can also be causal.

3.4. OMISSION AND INTENTION

While there is no difference between actions and omissions concerning the linkage element, this is not the case with respect to intention. I have argued that all positive actions have the feature of intentionality in the sense that what provokes the bodily movements is the intention to bring about a change, although whether an action is intentional depends on how it is interpreted. Where there is no such connection between an intention and bodily movements, i. e., between the internal and the external aspect of an action, we speak of reflex-acts rather than of actions. By contrast, it seems that we do speak of omissions even if there is no connection between an intention and the absence of certain bodily movements. What omission requires is that the action *could* be performed and that it is expected or obligatory, not that one must be aware of the omission when performing it.[15] That difference between actions and omissions can perhaps be explained by the greater weight of the social dimension in omissions, implying that the subjective dimension is less relevant.

3.5. OMISSION AND INTERPRETATION

[14] Garzón Valdés 1986, p. 27.

[15] That does not mean, however, that consciousness is not a requirement for the assessment of an omission as blameworthy. In fact, the question whether omissions must necessarily be voluntary is entirely parallel to the question whether actions must be voluntary. Perhaps it is convenient to distinguish between omissions and something like ‘reflex omissions’, in the same way as we distinguish between actions and ‘reflex acts’.

Finally, I think that one can say that omissions, just like actions, are phenomena with a meaning, that is, they entail an interpretation. To interpret an omission is to determine the change it has brought about as well as the change that was expected and did not come about. Such an interpretation can be done, once again, from a subjective, an intentional, or a social point of view.

An omission is interpreted intentionally, or from the agent's point of view, when it is believed that the omitted change is the change the agent intended to omit. Note that when an agent declares his intention of omitting to bring about a certain change this generates an expectation, in the sense of an inference that there must have been some reason for that change to be brought about in the first place. If I now declare my intention of omitting to take out a handkerchief, this suggests that there must be a reason why I had first thought to take out a handkerchief and then decided not to do so after all. Thus, I generate an expectation regarding that action.

From an observer's point of view – which in cases of omissions is the most frequent point of view adopted – the expectation indicating which action I omit can be due to at least three reasons. That is, there are at least three kinds of expectations regarding omissions:

(1) expectations based on obligations or duties: these are the most interesting for lawyers since legal omissions are of that kind; but it would be wrong to think that we speak of omissions only when some obligatory action is not performed;

(2) expectations based on behavioural regularities, either because of the agent's personality or because of sociological or psychological generalizations; and

(3) expectations based on the agent's rationality, where we can speak of an omission when the non-performance of an action seems irrational. Expectations based on technical rules can be included in this category.[16]

Once these different kinds of expectations are distinguished, we see that it is wrong to think that all omissions deserve a negative value-judgment, as has been held, for example, by Gimbernat.[17] This applies only to omissions generated by non-compliance with an obligation. Omissions based on irrational behaviour provoke judgments of irrationality, which I do not consider a kind of value-judgments. And those based on behavioural regularities are even compatible with a positive value-judgment: it makes perfect sense to say 'Fortunately, this time for once he omitted to do *x*'.

One conclusion to be drawn from all this is that, while the pattern of actions that has emerged in the previous chapters is readily applicable to institutional actions, it seems to fit less readily to omissions (for example, concerning the aspects of bodily movements and the link to an intention). Nevertheless, the parallels between omissions and positive actions can be regarded as sufficient to justify that the two are considered merely different modalities of human action or behaviour. In any case, what in my view is wrong is to link the question of whether or not there is a conceptual connection

[16] On the notion of 'technical rule', cf. von Wright 1963a, pp. 9 ff.

[17] Cf. Gimbernat Ordeig 1989, p. 579.

between positive actions and omissions to the question of whether or not omissions can support judgments of responsibility and blameworthiness. That seems to be a moral question concerning the acceptance of positive duties rather than the relationship between omissions and actions.

EPILOGUE

1. In the preceding pages, I have tried to offer an introduction to the theory of human action and, at the same time, to develop a position regarding some of the difficulties the reconstruction of that concept raises. I began by presenting some apparent contradictions between certain statements about actions which, taken in isolation, all seem intuitively acceptable. I have called the tension between the plausibility of these statements and their mutual inconsistency the 'paradoxes of action'. And I have suggested a way to dissolve that inconsistency – a way which is very common in analytical philosophy (though other approaches regard it as frustrating): by showing that those statements do not refer to one and the same concept of action, and that the word has different meanings in each of these statements. What are those meanings? It seems to me that the answer can be found if we review three 'battle lines' in the discussion about the concept of action (or in discussions where that concept forms part of the background): the analytical philosophy of action in the strict sense, the doctrine of criminal law, and the theory of speech acts. We have seen that the tension between, very roughly, actions understood as bodily movements or – in the case of speech acts – as a basic substrate, actions understood as the intentional meaning of what an agent has done, and actions understood as the social meaning, depending on social rules, of an agent's conduct is present in all three of them. And if we take into account this ambiguity of the term 'action', the inconsistency which gave rise to the paradoxes disappears. But not only do we have three different senses of one single word: it also seems that each one of them points to a dimension that is relevant for our understanding of actions. Those who emphasize bodily movements, for instance, do not deny the importance of action descriptions, and those who emphasize intention, or social rules, as the essential element of action likewise cannot deny that there must be a substrate on which the intentional or social interpretation operates. The ambiguity of the term 'action' arises precisely from taking one of these aspects – bodily movements, or intention, or the social meaning of an action – as the only one and identifying actions with it. Hence, the ambiguity results from the reduction of the concept of action to only one of the three dimensions.

In order to avoid such a reductionist attitude, we must look for a notion of action that encompasses all three dimensions. I have tried to approach such a notion, somewhat obliquely, through the analysis of what I have called the elements of action. If we look at the central cases of action, or at least at what philosophers and lawyers take them to be, we can distinguish at least five such elements, to wit: bodily movements, an intention, a change in the world, a relationship between the bodily movements and that change, and an interpretation or meaning of the action. The analysis undertaken in the preceding pages allows us to draw some conclusions about the relationships between these elements.

(1) Bodily movements are the element that enables us to link actions to the natural world. Actions are not merely descriptions, but always bodily movements onto which a description is hitched, that is, bodily movements interpreted in a certain way.

(2) Such bodily movements produce changes in the world, either causally or because there is some rule that correlates them (or some change causally produced by them) with an institutional change (that is, a change in the 'world' of norms, rules, conventions, institutions, etc.). If that kind of conventional generation of effects is accepted, we can account for institutional actions (i. e., for illocutionary speech acts as well as for many of the actions lawyers are concerned with).

(3) Among the different changes bodily movements can, causally or conventionally, produce, there is one that is intrinsic to the action in the sense that there is a conceptual relationship between the action and that change. I have called this change the 'action-internal change'. To say that there is a conceptual relationship between an action and a change does not imply that there is a third kind of change-production (although some authors do indeed speak of logical or conceptual generation, besides causal and conventional generation). We must not confuse the relationship between bodily movements (an element of action) and changes in the world with the relationship between an action as such and its action-internal change. That there is a logical relationship between an action and its action-internal change means that every type or class of actions is defined on the basis of a type or class of changes, such that if in a particular case the respective change is in fact not produced, one cannot say that the corresponding action has been performed. For example, the action of closing a door is defined by the change 'door open/door closed'. Hence, if such a change is not produced as a consequence of an agent's activity, an action of closing a door has not occured (although another action may have been performed, such as that of trying to close a door).

(4) I have suggested earlier that an action is not merely a bodily movement, nor is it only a description of such a bodily movement. Rather, it is something like a bodily movement *plus* (among other things) an interpretation of that bodily movement (an interpretation normally expressed in a certain description of the action). The interpretation of a bodily movement is a necessary operation in order to determine what kind of action has taken place (that is, to classify an act-token as an instance of a particular act-category). And since an action is defined on the basis of its action-internal change, that operation basically consists in choosing one of the changes produced by the bodily movements as the action-internal change.

(5) There are two kinds of interpretations of bodily movements. The first consists in adopting the intentional point of view, that is, trying to understand the action in the light of what the agent meant to do in performing the respective bodily movements. For such an interpretation, we must reconstruct the agent's intention (the action-internal change will then be the change the agent wanted to produce with his bodily movements). This is an operation which is sometimes very difficult and in which we can err. We must not forget that the purpose of the intentional interpretation of an action is that of 'discovering' an agent's mind-state, and that our interpretation may thus be true or false. The best intentional interpretation is the one that best reconstructs the agent's (real) intention. What criteria can we use for such interpretations? It is easier to give intentional interpretations of others' actions – we do it all the time – than to

answer that question. However, although I have hardly touched it in this book, I do think that it is a fundamental question for lawyers (linked to the problem of proving intent).

(6) The other kind of interpretation of bodily movements consists in considering them in the light of rules, conventions, and social practices. If any of the changes produced by the bodily movements in question seems relevant in that light, and if it also satisfies other prerequisites (if it is not too far removed in the causal chain, it it was foreseeable or should have been foreseen, etc.), it will be chosen by the observer as the action-internal change. In contrast to what happens in intentional interpretation, a non-intentional interpretation is given from a point of view external to the agent, his desires and intentions (though it may even be the agent himself who looks at his actions 'from the outside'). A non-intentional interpretation is correct to the extent that the criteria for choosing the action-internal change (relevance, length of the chain, foreseeability, etc.) are well-applied in the case at hand. It is a matter of ascribing rather than of 'discovering' an action-internal change. Besides, while in intentional interpretations the authority – at least a *prima facie* authority – is with the agent (which does not mean, of course, that we should always *believe* him), this is not the case with non-intentional interpretations.

(7) The distinction between intentional and non-intentional actions can be seen as deriving from these two kinds of interpretation of bodily movements. An intentional action is a bodily movement that is interpreted intentionally; a non-intentional action is a bodily movement that is interpreted non-intentionally. But both kinds of actions have an intention as one of their elements, which is not the case in involuntary actions (which philosophers and lawyers usually regard as actions only in a spurious sense). Intention is what sets in motion the bodily movements, and it is that link between intention and movements what we call voluntariness (in one of its senses).

(8) If we now extend the analysis of the elements of action to omissions, we find that there the social aspect is predominant. The determination of an 'omission-internal change' depends on what change was *expected* to be brought about, and that expectation in turn depends on practices and rules (social rules, rules of rationality, etc.). As in the case of non-intentional actions, determining whether an agent has omitted to perform an action is a matter of the application of rules and criteria (i. e., an ascription) rather than the description of a natural reality. There is a certain parallel between non-intentional actions and omissions: a non-intentional action can – if not always, at least sometimes – be regarded as the production of an unexpected or unrequired change; an omission, in turn, can be seen as the non-production of an expected or required change. The distinction between actions (in the broad sense) that are imputed or ascribed (non-intentional actions and omissions) and actions that are described (intentional actions) seems fundamental for a theory of legal evidence.

2. In his book *How to do things with Words*, John L. Austin denounced a fallacy concerning an attitude and a set of beliefs. As readers will know, the treatment of sentences or statements in the philosophy of language immediately preceding Austin's writing suffered from a defective approach: statements were analysed as if they all expressed true or false propositions about the world, that is, as if they were all descriptive; the existence of other functions of language was neglected. Austin contributed much to

show that this inadequate approach left a large and important subject area for philosophers in the dark, and he qualified the attitude of his contemporary colleagues as plagued by a „descriptive fallacy“.[1]

It has often seemed to me that continental legal theory in general (and by that I mean its non-Anglosaxon European branch as well as its Latin American branch) commits a fallacy that is somewhat similar to the one denounced by Austin. I would call it the 'normativistic fallacy'. It consists in acting as if the fundamental problems of legal theory were almost exclusively posed by norms and normative systems: the concept, the structure and the kinds of norms, the characteristics of normative systems, the dynamic aspects of the law, problems of interpretation, etc., are matters that have to do with norms, and they have been occupying most of our attention. But there is also another cluster of problems, rather independent of the former, concerning facts[2] and which seems no less important to me. Some examples of this second type of problems are the following: Which classes of facts are the most relevant for law? How can we know those facts? How are facts related to norms? What is an action? And what an omission? When is there only one, and when are there several actions? How can we determine whether there is a causal relationship between two events? Are facts objective and neutral, or are they 'theory-laden'? What consequences does this have for proving a fact in court? Can we really tell apart a *quaestio iuris* from a *quaestio facti*? How should we argue about matters of fact? When is there sufficient evidence for a fact (more precisely, for a statement about a fact)? How can we prove statements about 'mental facts', such as 'Peter had no intention to kill', or 'There was a certain hostility between Peter and John'? What 'motivates' a decision about what the proven facts are?

The relevance of these questions for an understanding of the operation of the law is fundamental. So much so that it is perhaps even justified to ask for a 'theory of facts' as part of the theory of law – a theory that tries to give answers to those questions and that is conceded the same rank as the 'theory of norms' or the 'theory of legal systems'.

I hope that this book will be seen as a contribution to such a 'theory of facts', and that it succeeds in drawing the attention of legal philosophers from a continental legal culture to that branch of legal philosophy – if only for the criticism it may deserve.

[1] John L. Austin 1976, p. 3.

[2] I use the expression 'fact' in the legal sense, encompassing actions (and intentions, emotions, etc.), and not in the sense of some philosophers who take facts (unterstood as events that are independent of the human will) as opposed to actions.

BIBLIOGRAPHY

ACERO, Juan José, Eduardo BUSTOS and Daniel QUESADA 1982: Introducción a la filosofía del lenguaje, Madrid: Cátedra.

AGUILÓ REGLA, Josep 2000: Teoría general de las fuentes del Derecho (y del orden jurídico, Barcelona: Ariel.

ALCHOURRÓN, Carlos 1986: Systematization and Change in the Science of Law, in: T. Eckhoff, L. Friedman and J. Uusitalo (eds.), Vernunft und Erfahrung im Rechtsdenken der Gegenwart (Rechtstheorie, Beiheft 10), Berlin: Duncker & Humblot, 171-184.

ANSCOMBE, G. E. M. 1963: Intention (1957), 2nd ed. Oxford: Basil Blackwell.

ATIENZA, Manuel 1984: Para una teoría general de la acción penal, in: Anuario de Derecho Penal, Madrid, 5-14.

ATIENZA, Manuel and Juan RUIZ MANERO 1998: A Theory of Legal Sentences, Dordrecht: Kluwer.

AUSTIN, J. L. 1976: How to do things with Words (1955), ed. by J. O. Urmson and M. Sbisà, 2nd ed. Oxford: Oxford University Press.

AUSTIN, J. L. 1979a: A plea for excuses, in: id., Philosophical Papers, ed. by J. O. Urmson and G. J. Warnock, 3rd ed. Oxford: Oxford University Press, 175-204 [first published in: Proceedings of the Aristotelian Society, 1956-7].

AUSTIN, J. L. 1979b: Other minds, in: id., Philosophical Papers, ed. by J. O. Urmson and G. J. Warnock, 3rd ed. Oxford: Oxford University Press, 76-116 [first published in: Proceedings of the Aristotelian Society, Supplementary volume XX, 1946].

AUSTIN, J. L. 1979c: Performative Utterances (1956), in: id., Philosophical Papers, ed. by J. O. Urmson and G. J. Warnock, 3rd ed. Oxford: Oxford University Press, 233-271.

BECHTEL, William 1988: Philosophy of Mind. An Overview for Cognitive Science, Hillsdale, N. J.: Erlbaum.

BERNSTEIN, Richard J. 1971: Praxis and Action, Philadelphia: University of Pennsylvania Press.

BRODBECK, May 1968: Meaning and Action, in: id. (ed.), Readings in the Philosophy of the Social Sciences, New York: Macmillan, London: Collier-Macmillan, 58-78.

BULYGIN, Eugenio 1986: Legal Dogmatics and the Systematization of Law, in: T. Eckhoff, L. Friedman and J. Uusitalo (eds.), Vernunft und Erfahrung im Rechtsdenken der Gegenwart (Rechtstheorie, Beiheft 10), Berlin: Duncker & Humblot, 193-210.

BUSTOS, Eduardo 1997: Acción humana y lingüística: La producción del sentido, in: M. Cruz (ed.), Acción humana, Barcelona: Ariel.

CARRIÓ, Genaro R. 1972: Prólogo, in: Carlos S. Nino, El concurso en el Derecho penal, Buenos Aires: Astrea.

CASTAÑEDA, Héctor Neri 1979: Intentionality and Identity in Human Action and Philosophical Method, in: Nous 1.

COBO DEL ROSAL, M. and T. VIVES ANTÓN 1984: Derecho penal. Parte general, Valencia: Universidad de Valencia.

CRUZ, Manuel 1990: Origen y desembocadura de la acción: El sujeto inevitable, in: Crítica (Mexico-City) XXII:64 (April).

DANTO, Arthur C. 1968: Basic Actions (1965), in: Alan R. White (ed.), The Philosophy of Action, Oxford: Oxford University Press, 43-58.

DAVIDSON, Donald 1980: Essays on Actions and Events, Oxford: Clarendon.

DAVIDSON, Donald 1980a: Agency (1971), in: id. 1980, 43-61.

DAVIDSON, Donald 1980b: The Individuation of Events (1969), in: id. 1980, 163-180.

DAVIDSON, Donald 1980c: The Logical Form of Action Sentences (1967), in: id. 1980, 105-122.

DAVIDSON, Donald 1980d: Intending (1978), in: id. 1980, 83-102.

DUFF, R. A. 1993: Acting, Trying, and Criminal Liability, in: Shute/Gardner/Horder (eds.) 1993, 75-106.

ELSTER, John 1983: Sour Grapes. Studies in the Subversion of Rationality, Cambridge et al.: Cambridge University Press, and Paris: Maison des Sciences de l'Homme.

FARRELL, Martín D. 1983: Utilitarismo. Etica y Politica, Buenos Aires: Abeledo-Perrot.

FEINBERG, Joel 1968: Action and responsibility (1965), in: Alan R. White (ed.), The Philosophy of Action, Oxford: Oxford University Press, 95-119.

FEINBERG, Joel 1988: Harm to Others. The Moral Limits of the Criminal Law, Oxford: Oxford University Press.

FITZGERALD, P. J. 1968: Voluntary and involuntary acts, in: White (ed.) 1968, 120-143.

FLETCHER, George P. 1998: Basic Concepts of Criminal Law, New York and Oxford: Oxford University Press.

GARCÍA SUÁREZ, Alfonso 1997: Modos de significar, Ed. Tecnos, Madrid.

GARZÓN VALDÉS, Ernesto 1970: Derecho y naturaleza de las cosas, 2 vols., Córdoba (Argentina): Universidad Nacional de Córdoba.

GARZÓN VALDÉS, Ernesto: Los deberes positivos generales y su fundamentación, in: Doxa (Alicante) 3, 17-33.

GIMBERNAT ORDEIG, Enrique 1989: Sobre los conceptos de omisión y comportamiento, in: Anuario de Derecho Penal (Madrid) Vol. XL, Fasc. III, 579-607..

GIMBERNAT ORDEIG, Enrique 1990: Delitos cualificados por el resultado y causalidad, Madrid: Centro de Estudios Ramón Areces.

GINET, Carl 1990: On Action, Cambridge: Cambridge University Press.

GOLDMAN, Alvin I. 1971: The Individuation of Action, in: The Journal of Philosophy LXVIII:21, 761-774.

GOLDMAN, Alvin I. 1976: A Theory of Human Action, Princeton, N. J.: Princeton University Press.

GÓMEZ BENÍTEZ, José Manuel 1988: Causalidad, imputación y cualificación por el resultado, Madrid: Ministerio de Justicia.

GONZÁLEZ LAGIER, Daniel 1993: Clasificar acciones. Sobre la crítica de Raz a las reglas constitutivas de Searle, in: DOXA (Alicante) 13.

GONZÁLEZ LAGIER, Daniel 1994: Sobre el concepto de causa, in: Poder Judicial 33.

GONZÁLEZ LAGIER, Daniel 1995: Acción y norma en G. H. von Wright, Madrid: Centro de Estudios Constitucionales.

GONZÁLEZ LAGIER, Daniel 1997: Cómo hacer cosas con acciones. Sobre las reglas de acción y las reglas de fin, in: Doxa (Alicante) 20.

GRICE, H. P. 1971: Utterer's Meaning, Sentence-Meaning, and Word-Meaning (1967), in: John R. Searle (ed.), The Philosophy of Language, Oxford: Oxford University Press, 54-70.

GRICE, H. P. 1989a: Utterer's Meaning and Intentions (1967), in: id., Studies in the Way of Words, Cambridge, Mass.: Harvard University Press, 86-116.

GRICE, H. P. 1989b: Meaning (1948, 1957), in: id., Studies in the Way of Words, Cambridge, Mass.: Harvard University Press, 213-223.

GUIBOURG, Ricardo A. 1987: El fenómeno normativo, Buenos Aires: Astrea.

HABERMAS, Jürgen: Theorie des kommunikativen Handelns, 2 vols., Frankfurt a. M.: Suhrkamp 1988.

HAMPSHIRE, S. and H. L. A. HART 1958.: Decision, Intention and Certainty, in: Mind LXVII:265.

HART, H. L. A. 1948/49: The Ascription of Responsibility and Rights, in: Proceedings of the Aristotelian Society 49, 145-166.

HART, H. L. A. 1973: Punishment and Responsibility, Oxford: Clarendon.

HART, H. L. A. and A. M. HONORÉ 1959: Causation in the Law, Oxford: Clarendon.

HIERRO S. PESCADOR, José 1982: Principios de filosofía del lenguaje. 2. Teoría del significado, Madrid: Alianza.

HUME, David 1975: An Enquiry Concerning Human Understanding, in: Enquiries Concerning Human Understanding and Concerning the Principles of Morals, reprinted from the posthumous edition of 1777 and edited with Introduction, Comparative Table of Contents, and Analytical Index by L. A. Selby-Bigge, 3rd ed., with text revised and notes by P. H. Nidditch, Oxford: Clarendon.

JAÉN VALLEJO, Manuel 1994: El concepto de acción en la dogmática penal, Madrid: Colex.

LARRAÑAGA MONJARAZ, Pablo (2000): El concepto de responsabilidad, Mexico-City: Fontamara.

MARDONES, J. M. 1991: Filosofía de las ciencias humanas y sociales. Nota histórica de una polémica incesante, in: id. (ed.), Filosofía de las ciencias humanas y sociales. Materiales para una fundamentación científica, Barcelona: Anthropos.

MOORE, Michael S. 1993: Act and Crime, Oxford: Clarendon.

MOSTERÍN, Jesús 1983: Racionalidad y acción humana, Madrid: Alianza.

MOYA, Carlos J. 1990: The Philosophy of Action. An Introduction, Cambridge: Polity Press.

NAGEL, Ernest 1961: The Structure of Science, New York: Harcourt, Brace & World.

NINO, Carlos S. 1972: El concurso en el Derecho Penal, Buenos Aires: Astrea.

NINO, Carlos S. 1980: Los límites de la responsabilidad penal, Buenos Aires: Astrea.

NINO, Carlos S. 1987: Introducción a la filosofía de la acción humana, Buenos Aires: Eudeba.

OGDEN, C. K. and I. A. RICHARDS: The Meaning of Meaning. A Study of the Influence of Language Upon Thought and of the Science of Symbolism (1923), New York: Harcourt, Brace & World.

PUIG BRUTAU, J. 1950-1993: Hecho jurídico, in: C. E. Mascareñas y B. Pellisé Prats (eds.), Nueva Enciclopedia Jurídica, Barcelona: Francisco Seix.

RABOSSI, Eduardo A. 1997: La filosofía de la acción y la filosofía de la mente, in: Manuel Cruz (ed.), Acción humana, Barcelona: Ariel.

RAZ, Joseph 1990: Practical Reason and Norms (1975), Princeton, N. J.: Princeton University Press.

REDONDO, María Cristina: Reasons for Action and the Law, Dordrecht: Kluwer 1999.

RODRÍGUEZ MOURULLO, Gonzalo 1966: La omisión de socorro en el código penal, Madrid: Tecnos.

RYLE, Gilbert 1949: The Concept of Mind, London: Hutchinson.

SEARLE, John R. 1969: Speech Acts. An Essay in the Philosophy of Language, Cambridge: Cambridge University Press.

SEARLE, John R. 1971: What is a speech-act?, in: id. (ed.), The Philosophy of Language, Oxford: Oxford University Press, 39-53 [first published in: Max Black (ed.), Philosophy in America, London: Allen & Unwin 1965, 221-239].

SEARLE, John R. 1979a: A Taxonomy of Illocutionary Acts, in: id., Expression and Meaning: Studies in the Theory of Speech Acts, Cambridge: Cambridge University Press, 1-29.

SEARLE, John R. 1979b: Indirect Speech Acts (1974), in: id., Expression and Meaning: Studies in the Theory of Speech Acts, Cambridge: Cambridge University Press, 30-57.

SEARLE, John R. 1983: Intentionality. An Essay in the Philosophy of Mind, Cambridge: Cambridge University Press.

SEARLE, John R. 1984: Minds, Brains and Science: The 1984 Reith Lectures, Cambridge, Mass.: Harvard University Press.

SEARLE, John R. 1992: The Rediscovery of the Mind, Cambridge, Mass.: MIT Press.

SHUTE, Stephen, John GARDNER and Jeremy HORDER 1993: Introduction: The Logic of Criminal Law, in: id. (eds.) 1993, 1-20.

SHUTE, Stephen, John GARDNER and Jeremy HORDER (eds.) 1993: Action and Value in Criminal Law, Oxford: Clarendon.

SIMPSON, Thomas Moro 1985: El fantasma de la máquina: Notas sobre dualismo y materialismo, in: Análisis Filosófico 5:2, 57-66.

STRAWSON, Peter F. 1974: Freedom and Resentment, in: id., *Freedom and Resentment* and other essays, London: Methuen.

TUR, Richard H. S. 1993: Subjectivism and Objectivism: Toward Synthesis, in: Shute/ Gardner/Horder (eds.) 1993, 213-237.

VALDÉS VILLANUEVA, Luis M. 1978: Significado y actos de habla. Un estudio de lógica filosófica, Ph. D. Diss., University of Valencia, Spain (unpublished manuscript).

VIVES ANTÓN, Tomás 1996: Fundamentos del Sistema Penal, Valencia: Tirant Lo Blanch.

WAISMANN, Friedrich 1968: How I see philosophy (1956), in: id., How I See Philosophy, ed. R. Harré, London: Macmillan, 1-38.

WELZEL, Hans 1947: Das Deutsche Strafrecht, 1st ed. Berlin: Walter de Gruyter.

WELZEL, Hans 1951: Naturrecht und materiale Gerechtigkeit, Göttingen: Vandenhoeck und Ruprecht.

WELZEL, Hans 1961: Das neue Bild des Strafrechtssystems. Eine Einführung in die finale Handlungslehre, Göttingen: Schwartz.

WHITE, Alan R. 1985: Grounds of Liability, Oxford: Clarendon.

WHITE, Alan R. (ed.) 1968: The Philosophy of Action, Oxford: Oxford University Press.

WITTGENSTEIN, Ludwig 1958: Philosophical Investigations, Oxford: Basil Blackwell.

VON WRIGHT, Georg Henrik 1963a: Norm and Action, London: Routledge & Kegan Paul.

VON WRIGHT, Georg Henrik 1963b: The Varieties of Goodness, London: Routledge & Kegan Paul.

VON WRIGHT, Georg Henrik 1968: An Essay in Deontic Logic and the General Theory of Action (Acta Philosophica Fennica, Fasc. XXI), Amsterdam: North-Holland.

VON WRIGHT, Georg Henrik 1971: Explanation and Understanding, London: Routledge & Kegan Paul.

VON WRIGHT, Georg Henrik 1980: Freedom and Determination (Acta Philosophica Fennica, vol. XXXI, no. 1), Amsterdam: North-Holland.

VON WRIGHT, Georg Henrik 1983a: Determinism and the Study of Man, in: id., Philosophical Papers, vol. I: Practical Reason, Oxford: Basil Blackwell, 35-52 [first in: J. Manninen and R. Tuomela (eds.), Essays on Explanation and Understanding. Studies in the Formation of Humanities and Social Sciences, Dordrecht: D. Reidel, 415-435].

VON WRIGHT, Georg Henrik 1983b: On the Logic of Norms and Actions, in: id., Practical Reason, Philosophical Papers, vol. I, Oxford: Basil Blackwell, 100-129.

INDEX OF NAMES

Acero, J. J. *59*, *72*
Adorno, Th. 107
Aguiló Regla, J. *15*
Alchourrón, C. E. *46*
Anscombe, G. E. M. 24 ff., 74, 91, 99
Archduke Francis Ferdinand 23 ff., 85
Aristotle *9*, 44, 107 f.
Atienza, M. *9*, 10, *82*, *94*
Austin, J. 51
Austin, J. L. 2, 7 f., *9*, 10, 11, 57, 62-69, 72, 77, 81 f., 125 f.

Bechtel, W. *98*, *100*
Bentham, J. 13, 51
Berkeley, G. 15
Bernstein, R. J. 23
Brodbeck, M. 100
Bulygin, E. *46*
Bustos, E. 55, *56*, *59*, *72*, 109 f.

Carnap, R. 23
Carrió, G. R. 11
Castañeda, H. N. 29
Cobo del Rosal, M. *40*, *43*, 45
Copernicus, N. 46
Cruz, M. 84

Danto, A. C. *27*, 34, 37, 81
Davidson, D. 24 ff., 29 f., 36, 53, 88, 91, 103
Descartes 99, 101
Dennett, D. 19
Duff, R. A. *50*, 52
Durkheim, E. 41

Elster, J. 108

Farrell, M. D. *13*
Feinberg, J. 9, 21, 24, *27*, 33 ff., 53, 85, 96
Fitzgerald, P. J. 14
Fletcher, G. 9, 19, *119*

Galilei, G. 44, 107
García Suárez, A. *111*
Gardner, J. *9*
Garzón Valdés, E. *9*, 120
Geach, P. 33
Gimbernat Ordeig, E. *40*, 121
Ginet, C. *24*, 29, *30*
Goldman, A. I. 24-30, 35 f., 40, *97*, 101
Gómez Benítez, J. M. *43*
González Lagier, D. *71*, *90*, *95*, *96*, *97*
Grice, H. P. *47*, 57, 58-62, 69, 77
Guibourg, R. *9*, *13*, 112 f.

Habermas, J. 92, 107
Hampshire. St. 18
Hart, H. L. A. 9, 18, 19, 30, 32 ff., 36 f., 46, 50 f., *52*, 53, 79, 100, *105*
Hegel, G. W. F. 40 f., 43
Hierro S. Pescador, J. *56*, *57*, 59, *60*, 68, *74*
Holmes, O. W. 51, 53
Honoré, A. M. *9*
Horder, J. *9*
Hume, D. 15

Jaén Vallejo, M. *44*, *45*
Jescheck, H.-H. 45

Kant, I. 13
Kelman, M. 19
Kuhn, Th. 108

Lakatos, I. 108
Larrañaga Monjaraz, P. *34*
Leibniz, G. W. 111
von Liszt, F. 42

McCann, H. *27*
Mackie, J. L. 118
Maihofer, W. 40, 44 f.
Mardones, J. M. *44*, 107, *108*
Melden, A. I. 20, 100
Moore, M. S. 9, 14, 19, *20*, 22, 46, *50*, 51
Mosterín, J. 31 f., 36, 97, 108
Moya, C. J. *25*, *27*, 101 f., 104

Nagel, E. *96*
Nino, C. S. *9*, 11, *12*, *14*, 16, *17*, 21, 29, *33*, *39*, 49, *50*, 87 f., *99*, *106*, *118*

Ogden, C. K. 107

Peters, R. 20
Pitcher, G. 33
Popper, K. R. 107
Princip, G. 23 ff., 85
Puig Brutau, J. *14*

Quesada, D. *59*, *72*

Rabossi, E. A. *9*
Raz, J. *97*
Redondo, M. C. *94*
Richards, I. A. 107
Rodríguez Mourullo, G. *40*, *118*
Ross, A. *71*
Ruiz Manero, J. *82*, *94*
Russell, B. 107
Ryle, G. 99 f.

Schmidt, E. 45
Searle, J. R. *17*, 26, 47, *48*, 55, 57, *60*, 61 f., 69-77, *94*, 95, 97, 98, 100 f., 104 f., 115 ff.
Shute, St. *9*
Simpson, Th. M. *99*
Strawson, P. F. 16

Tur, R. H. S. 52

Valdés Villanueva, L. M. 62, *66*
Vives Antón, T. *9*, 40 ff., *43*, *44*, 45 ff., 53

Waismann, F. 7
Welzel, H. *9*, *42*, 43, 44
White, A. R. *105*
Wittgenstein, L. 7, 23, 47, 56 f., *62*, 69, 99 f., 107
von Wright, G. H. 4, 7, *9*, *12*, 13, *27*, 30 ff., 35 ff., *44*, 53, *71*, 79, 81, 84, 89, *96*, 102 f., 107 ff., *111*, 117 ff., *121*

Law and Philosophy Library

1. E. Bulygin, J.-L. Gardies and I. Niiniluoto (eds.): *Man, Law and Modern Forms of Life.* With an Introduction by M.D. Bayles. 1985 ISBN 90-277-1869-5
2. W. Sadurski: *Giving Desert Its Due.* Social Justice and Legal Theory. 1985 ISBN 90-277-1941-1
3. N. MacCormick and O. Weinberger: *An Institutional Theory of Law.* New Approaches to Legal Positivism. 1986 ISBN 90-277-2079-7
4. A. Aarnio: *The Rational as Reasonable.* A Treatise on Legal Justification. 1987 ISBN 90-277-2276-5
5. M.D. Bayles: *Principles of Law.* A Normative Analysis. 1987 ISBN 90-277-2412-1; Pb: 90-277-2413-X
6. A. Soeteman: *Logic in Law.* Remarks on Logic and Rationality in Normative Reasoning, Especially in Law. 1989 ISBN 0-7923-0042-4
7. C.T. Sistare: *Responsibility and Criminal Liability.* 1989 ISBN 0-7923-0396-2
8. A. Peczenik: *On Law and Reason.* 1989 ISBN 0-7923-0444-6
9. W. Sadurski: *Moral Pluralism and Legal Neutrality.* 1990 ISBN 0-7923-0565-5
10. M.D. Bayles: *Procedural Justice.* Allocating to Individuals. 1990 ISBN 0-7923-0567-1
11. P. Nerhot (ed.): *Law, Interpretation and Reality.* Essays in Epistemology, Hermeneutics and Jurisprudence. 1990 ISBN 0-7923-0593-0
12. A.W. Norrie: *Law, Ideology and Punishment.* Retrieval and Critique of the Liberal Ideal of Criminal Justice. 1991 ISBN 0-7923-1013-6
13. P. Nerhot (ed.): *Legal Knowledge and Analogy.* Fragments of Legal Epistemology, Hermeneutics and Linguistics. 1991 ISBN 0-7923-1065-9
14. O. Weinberger: *Law, Institution and Legal Politics.* Fundamental Problems of Legal Theory and Social Philosophy. 1991 ISBN 0-7923-1143-4
15. J. Wróblewski: *The Judicial Application of Law.* Edited by Z. Bańkowski and N. MacCormick. 1992 ISBN 0-7923-1569-3
16. T. Wilhelmsson: *Critical Studies in Private Law.* A Treatise on Need-Rational Principles in Modern Law. 1992 ISBN 0-7923-1659-2
17. M.D. Bayles: *Hart's Legal Philosophy.* An Examination. 1992 ISBN 0-7923-1981-8
18. D.W.P. Ruiter: *Institutional Legal Facts.* Legal Powers and their Effects. 1993 ISBN 0-7923-2441-2
19. J. Schonsheck: *On Criminalization.* An Essay in the Philosophy of the Criminal Law. 1994 ISBN 0-7923-2663-6
20. R.P. Malloy and J. Evensky (eds.): *Adam Smith and the Philosophy of Law and Economics.* 1994 ISBN 0-7923-2796-9
21. Z. Bańkowski, I. White and U. Hahn (eds.): *Informatics and the Foundations of Legal Reasoning.* 1995 ISBN 0-7923-3455-8
22. E. Lagerspetz: *The Opposite Mirrors.* An Essay on the Conventionalist Theory of Institutions. 1995 ISBN 0-7923-3325-X

Law and Philosophy Library

23. M. van Hees: *Rights and Decisions.* Formal Models of Law and Liberalism. 1995 ISBN 0-7923-3754-9
24. B. Anderson: *"Discovery" in Legal Decision-Making.* 1996 ISBN 0-7923-3981-9
25. S. Urbina: *Reason, Democracy, Society.* A Study on the Basis of Legal Thinking. 1996 ISBN 0-7923-4262-3
26. E. Attwooll: *The Tapestry of the Law.* Scotland, Legal Culture and Legal Theory. 1997 ISBN 0-7923-4310-7
27. J.C. Hage: *Reasoning with Rules.* An Essay on Legal Reasoning and Its Underlying Logic. 1997 ISBN 0-7923-4325-5
28. R.A. Hillman: *The Richness of Contract Law.* An Analysis and Critique of Contemporary Theories of Contract Law. 1997 ISBN 0-7923-4336-0; 0-7923-5063-4 (Pb)
29. C. Wellman: *An Approach to Rights.* Studies in the Philosophy of Law and Morals. 1997 ISBN 0-7923-4467-7
30. B. van Roermund: *Law, Narrative and Reality.* An Essay in Intercepting Politics. 1997 ISBN 0-7923-4621-1
31. I. Ward: *Kantianism, Postmodernism and Critical Legal Thought.* 1997 ISBN 0-7923-4745-5
32. H. Prakken: *Logical Tools for Modelling Legal Argument.* A Study of Defeasible Reasoning in Law. 1997 ISBN 0-7923-4776-5
33. T. May: *Autonomy, Authority and Moral Responsibility.* 1998 ISBN 0-7923-4851-6
34. M. Atienza and J.R. Manero: *A Theory of Legal Sentences.* 1998 ISBN 0-7923-4856-7
35. E.A. Christodoulidis: *Law and Reflexive Politics.* 1998 ISBN 0-7923-4954-7
36. L.M.M. Royakkers: *Extending Deontic Logic for the Formalisation of Legal Rules.* 1998 ISBN 0-7923-4982-2
37. J.J. Moreso: *Legal Indeterminacy and Constitutional Interpretation.* 1998 ISBN 0-7923-5156-8
38. W. Sadurski: *Freedom of Speech and Its Limits.* 1999 ISBN 0-7923-5523-7
39. J. Wolenski (ed.): *Kazimierz Opalek Selected Papers in Legal Philosophy.* 1999 ISBN 0-7923-5732-9
40. H.P. Visser 't Hooft: *Justice to Future Generations and the Environment.* 1999 ISBN 0-7923-5756-6
41. L.J. Wintgens (ed.): *The Law in Philosophical Perspectives.* My Philosophy of Law. 1999 ISBN 0-7923-5796-5
42. A.R. Lodder: *DiaLaw.* On Legal Justification and Dialogical Models of Argumentation. 1999 ISBN 0-7923-5830-9
43. C. Redondo: *Reasons for Action and the Law.* 1999 ISBN 0-7923-5912-7
44. M. Friedman, L. May, K. Parsons and J. Stiff (eds.): *Rights and Reason.* Essays in Honor of Carl Wellman. 2000 ISBN 0-7923-6198-9

Law and Philosophy Library

45. G.C. Christie: *The Notion of an Ideal Audience in Legal Argument.* 2000
ISBN 0-7923-6283-7
46. R.S. Summers: *Essays in Legal Theory.* 2000 ISBN 0-7923-6367-1
47. M. van Hees: *Legal Reductionism and Freedom.* 2000 ISBN 0-7923-6491-0
48. R. Gargarella: *The Scepter of Reason.* Public Discussion and Political Radicalism in the Origins of Constitutionalism. 2000 ISBN 0-7923-6508-9
49. M. Iglesias Vila: *Facing Judicial Discretion.* Legal Knowledge and Right Answers Revisited. 2001 ISBN 0-7923-6778-2
50. M. Kiikeri: *Comparative Legal Reasoning and European Law.* 2001 ISBN 0-7923-6884-3
51. A.J. Menéndez: *Justifying Taxes.* Some Elements for a General Theory of Democratic Tax Law. 2001 ISBN 0-7923-7052-X
52. W.E. Conklin: *The Invisible Origins of Legal Positivism.* A Re-Reading of a Tradition. 2001
ISBN 0-7923-7101-1
53. Z. Bańkowski: *Living Lawfully.* Love in Law and Law in Love. 2001 ISBN 0-7923-7180-1
54. A.N. Shytov: *Conscience and Love in Making Judicial Decisions.* 2001
ISBN 1-4020-0168-1
55. D.W.P. Ruiter: *Legal Institutions.* 2001 ISBN 1-4020-0186-X
56. D.G. Lagier: *The Paradoxes of Action.* (Human Action, Law and Philosophy). 2003 ISBN 1-4020-1661-1

Volumes 56–63 were published by Kluwer Law International.

57. G. den Hartogh: *Mutual Expectations.* A Conventionalist Theory of Law. 2002
ISBN 90-411-1796-2
58. W.L. Robison (ed.): *The Legal Essays of Michael Bayles.* 2002 ISBN 90-411-1835-7
59. U. Bindreiter: *Why Grundnorm?* A Treatise on the Implications of Kelsen's Doctrine. 2002
ISBN 90-411-1867-5
60. S. Urbina: *Legal Method and the Rule of Law.* 2002 ISBN 90-411-1870-5
61. M. Baurmann: *The Market of Virtue.* Morality and Commitment in a Liberal Society. 2002
ISBN 90-411-1874-8
62. G. Zanetti: *Political Friendship and the Good Life.* Two Liberal Arguments against Perfectionism. 2002 ISBN 90-411-1881-0
63. W. Sadurski (ed.): *Constitutional Justice, East and West.* 2002 ISBN 90-411-1883-7
64. S. Taekema: *The Concept of Ideals in Legal Theory.* 2003 ISBN 90-411-1971-X
65. J. Raitio: *The Principle of Legal Certainty in EC Law.* 2003 ISBN 1-4020-1217-9
66. E. Santoro: *Individual Autonomy, Freedom and Rights.* 2003 ISBN 1-4020-1404-X
67. D. González Lagier: *The Paradoxes of Action.* (Human Action, Law and Philosophy). 2003
ISBN Hb-1-4020-1661-1

KLUWER ACADEMIC PUBLISHERS – DORDRECHT / BOSTON / NEW YORK

MIX
Papier aus verantwortungsvollen Quellen
Paper from responsible sources
FSC® C105338

If you have any concerns about our products,
you can contact us on
ProductSafety@springernature.com

In case Publisher is established outside the EU,
the EU authorized representative is:
Springer Nature Customer Service Center GmbH
Europaplatz 3, 69115 Heidelberg, Germany

Printed by Libri Plureos GmbH
in Hamburg, Germany